D0114036

THE COLLEGE EXPERIENCE

by

Mervin B.

Freedman

THE COLLEGE EXPERIENCE

Jossey-Bass Inc., Publishers

615 Montgomery Street · San Francisco · 1967

THE COLLEGE EXPERIENCE
by Mervin B. Freedman

Jossey-Bass, Inc., Publishers
615 Montgomery Street
San Francisco, California 94111

Library of Congress Catalog
Card Number 67-13280

Printed in the United States of America
by York Composition Company, Inc.
York, Pennsylvania

6734

THE JOSSEY-BASS BEHAVIORAL SCIENCE SERIES

William E. Henry, General Editor

To

Marjorie

Preface

College and university experience can give to many millions of young people the sense of being truly alive. In the words of Joseph Conrad, it may speak "to our capacity for delight and wonder, to the sense of mystery surrounding our lives; to our sense of pity, and beauty, and pain; to the latent feeling of fellowship with all creation . . . to the solidarity in dreams, in joy, in sorrow, in aspirations, in illusions, in hope, in fear, which binds . . . together all humanity."[1] College and university bulletins and catalogues lay claim to accomplishments of this kind. I am persuaded that the claims are sometimes justified, that colleges can and sometimes do give young people such a sense of life. With increased knowledge of students and of the workings of colleges and universities this can be done more often. This is the essential message of *The College Experience.*

The college years are a prime educational period. College students are in a stage of personality development that permits expansion of the intellect and of the personality in ways that are not possible during the secondary school years. It is likely that never again in their lifetimes will students be so free and open to new experience. Moreover, research reported in this book indicates that

[1] As quoted in Muller, Herbert J. *The Spirit of Tragedy.* New York: Knopf, 1956, p. 333.

the changes that occur during the college years have considerable persistence. At age seventy-five one is likely to hold many of the values and attitudes held at age twenty-two.

College education can make an enormous contribution to individuals and to society, but if this is to happen, barriers both within and without the colleges that stand in the way must be broken down. In *The College Experience* I explicate some of the barriers to realization of the full potentiality of higher education. Military service for young men, for example, has received considerable attention. The issue of whether college students in good standing should be deferred is obviously of great ethical and political significance. What is generally overlooked, however, is the way in which the draft has suppressed certain kinds of development in youth, that is, a tendency for young people in our society to take a long time before committing themselves to careers and ways of life. I support such an experimental approach to life on the basis that those people who are going the farthest are likely to take the longest time to get there. This kind of development is appropriate to an affluent society in which there is little place for youth in the work force. The tendency among students to interrupt their formal education from time to time to work, to travel, to contemplate, to "hack around," was burgeoning a few years ago. This kind of interruption of education, which consists essentially in changing the setting for education, has become a casualty of the Vietnamese war. The draft is stifling American society by preventing variety of experience and tentativeness of commitment which should be part of development in an affluent and post-industrial world.

Another barrier to true education is pedantry and formalism. Concerning student unrest and rebelliousness I have written: "It should be apparent . . . that demands for more and more effort from youth, intense competition among them, and the necessity that they choose their major field of study and define themselves vocationally and professionally earlier and earlier can lead only to the empty, joyless life of Blake's vision." The hostility to liberal education of certain segments of American society is another formidable barrier, and I have written: "I foresee many conflicts—over Vietnam, over the draft, over civil rights, over the use of drugs, and many other issues. In these conflicts faculty members and students will have some allies: liberal politicians and clergymen, for example. But by and large most of American society will be arrayed against them. This discord could become very intense." Unhappily, the current political situation in California confirms these forewarnings.

The college years demarcate a stage of personality development which I view from psychological and sociological perspectives. I portray the majority of college students as unsophisticated, conventional, and stable, rather more in need of being stirred up than calmed down—in contrast to the views of many psychiatrists and psychologists who depict the college years as a seething caldron of neurosis and emotional turbulence. When students do experience emotional difficulties, I consider Sigmund Freud's model of neurosis, the ego caught between the demands of anarchic impulse and rigid conscience, to be as apposite for middle-class youth today as in 1900. I challenge the ubiquitousness during the college years of what has been termed "the search for identity."

The research on which this book is based has kept me in close touch with college and university students for almost fifteen years. There is much to be learned from the process of studying youth. One may see the evolutionary process at work, the future outlined. Youth are preparing for a different human and social condition. In *The College Experience* I have delineated certain of these trends: restoration of unity of the personality and of the intellect; establishment of the ethic of social service as a powerful force in individual and social life; revival of eroticism (what Henry Murray calls the "erotic imagination"); and restitution of a sense of community to colleges and universities and other institutions of society. No facet of individual and social existence will be untouched by these directions youth are taking. My speculations concerning the future of Western civilization based on studies of students have much in common with Robert Theobald's predictions based on analysis of economic phenomena and with Marshall McLuhan's predictions based on scrutiny of mass media.

Since I am a psychologist, I have written with other psychologists and behavioral and social scientists very much in mind. I have tried, in addition, to address readers who may not have specialized knowledge in the behavioral and social sciences—educators, college and university students, and the parents of students, for example. If this book contributes even in a small way to realization of the enormous individual and social potential of higher education, I shall be rewarded.

In writing *The College Experience* I have been aware of my indebtedness to many persons and institutions. To Nevitt Sanford of Stanford University, my mentor in graduate school and friend and colleague for many years, my debts are great. His ability to grasp the fundament of a social problem, to see research issues in the widest theoretical perspective, to explicate the human relevance of intellectual and academic concerns has been inspirational to me. I owe much as well to Harold Webster of the City University of New York. Over the years his friendship has been very important to me, and he has contributed to my store of psychological knowledge, in particular, knowledge of research design and methods for analysis of data. Professor Webster read the entire manuscript and made valuable emendations.

I am indebted to Vassar College and its Mary Conover Mellon Foundation for the Advancement of Education. Studies of college and university students are commonplace now; but in 1952, when the research reported in this book was begun at Vassar, such studies were a rarity indeed. The faculty and administration of Vassar displayed uncommon openness and courage in permitting my colleagues and me to investigate systematically what it was like to matriculate at Vassar College. I wish to thank President Emeritus Sarah Gibson Blanding and Miss Gertrude Garnsey, Mrs. Florence Wislocki, Mrs. Mary Meeker Gesek, and Mrs. Tania Goss Morgan, all of Vassar College, for encouragement and support.

I began to write this book in the year I spent as a Fellow of the Center for Advanced Study in the Behavioral Sciences, Stanford, California. The leisure and intellectual stimulation afforded by the Center provided me with glimpses of the wider implications of the empirical research in which I had been engaged. I am grateful to Ralph Tyler, Preston Cutler, and Jane Kielsmeier of the

Center for all that they did to make possible so valuable and enjoyable a year.

Parts of this book were written at the Institute of Educational Research of the University of Oslo, where I spent a year as a Fulbright Research Scholar, and at the Tavistock Institute in London. Conversations with Professor Johannes Sandven and Professor Per Rand of the University of Oslo and Mr. Eric Trist of the Tavistock Institute helped to expand my educational and psychological horizons.

This book owes much to my association at various times during its writing with the following colleagues: Carl Bereiter (who helped with the research reported in Chapter 5), Richard Jung, Christian Bay, Joseph Katz, Max Levin, Robert Wert, Robert Hind, Harvey Powelson (who helped formulate the opinions and observations expressed in Chapter 12), Robert Suczek, Paul Kanzer, Winslow Hatch, Donald Brown, Elizabeth Alfert, Joseph Axelrod, and Donal Jones. I have received research assistance from Lillian Eisberg, Ellen Mendel, John Bryson, Rey Carr, Tupper Pettit, Mallory Jones, Roger Squire, and Molly Sterling, and clerical assistance from Barbara Glover, Nancy Halderman, Diane Borden, Mildred Tubby, Phyllis Merritt, and Elfriede Rascher. My thanks to all.

Last but hardly least I should like to express my gratitude to the students of Vassar, Stanford, California, Mills College, and San Francisco State, and the alumnae of Vassar who have served as subjects in the research reported in this book. It would give me great pleasure to learn that some former research subjects read this book and considered their contributions of time and effort to have been worthwhile.

Mervin B. Freedman

Berkeley, California
February, 1967

Contents

THE COLLEGE EXPERIENCE

I

THE COLLEGE AND SOCIETY

1

The College and Social Change

When college administrators and faculty members talk about higher education, two divergent points of view emerge. There is, on the one hand, a stream of rhetoric about the virtues and rewards of college education. Liberal education will make students more independent in their judgment and more flexible in their thinking; it will make them more aware of themselves and of the world around them; it will make them less prejudiced in their thinking; it will make them more socially responsible. Liberal education will, in short, save men's souls and the world.

There is also the darker and more pessimistic view. This is the notion that college experience does nothing at all for students—or next to nothing. In this crass, material world the philistines are obviously winning out, and higher education is palpably incapable of stemming the tide. Often faculty members actually seem to enjoy sentiments of this kind. Sometimes they revel in them. I believe that many intellectuals derive masochistic satisfaction from a feeling of isolation from the mainstream of American life and from the sense that they are a beleaguered minority group.[1] This is one of the reasons for the popularity of Philip Jacob's book, *Changing Values in College,*[2] among college faculty members. Jacob asserted that, with the exception of a few colleges, relatively small colleges which contained a number of faculty members with deeply idealistic convictions and commitments, college experience exerted almost no influence on the values of students. I have heard many a faculty member report this finding—almost with a feeling of glee, it seemed.

Both these views are wide of the mark. It is true that college attendance does not produce dramatic changes in most students. How could it be otherwise, given the close association between colleges and universities in the United States and the society at large? Most colleges and universities are financially beholden to the federal government for scholarships, buildings, and research grants. State and municipal institutions depend upon the good will and the votes of aldermen, state legislators, and the citizenry at large. Private colleges and universities and public institutions as well need the support of alumni, parents, and business and industry.

Obviously the viability of colleges and universities requires they not be too alienated from the wider society in which they are embedded. Society's pressures are often subtle, but they are there; and they are powerful. Faculty members in fields which encompass social criticism—literature, history, or sociology, for example—are aware that their lectures are often altered when parents are present in a class, as on a visitors' day. The college president who avows publicly that his students have the right to engage in movements of social protest will privately assuage an outraged Southern trustee by informing him that only a handful of students are actively involved in the civil rights movement. The student who goes home at Christmas or who is applying for a position in a large corporation is aware of many subtle pressures. He may not bow overtly to these

[1] Intellectuals are not nearly so powerless to influence American culture as many of them seem to think. Their writings have considerable impact on the American scene. The influence of pediatricians, psychologists, and psychiatrists on child-rearing practices in the United States is a good example.

[2] Jacob, Philip E. *Changing Values in College.* New York: Harper, 1957.

pressures, but they are likely to influence him, often in ways of which he is not fully aware.

Thus the expectation that college experience will exert a marked impact on large numbers of students, that many thousands of Thoreaus and Melvilles will be graduated from American campuses every June, is completely unreasonable. No society will tolerate an institution that so effectively undermines its values. A college which actually turned out large numbers of graduates who approximated the ideal of the educated person as described in the college catalogue would soon be in trouble with legislators, donors, and parents.[3]

On the other hand, few students pass through college completely untouched by liberalizing influences. The outcome of college education is likely to be a compromise between the characteristics of entering freshmen, most of whom are exponents of the conventional middle-class values and outlook on life, and the ideals of liberal education. Most freshmen are indeed changed by the time of graduation, though not greatly changed.

Educators and liberal critics of American higher education are bothered by the relatively small amount of change that takes place in students. They see this as evidence of the ineffectiveness of American colleges. They look at individual students or alumni, observe that they have changed but little, and throw up their hands in despair. This reaction is a misperception of the way in which social change takes place. The key to social change is that, in a dynamic system, slight changes in individuals can lead to profound changes in the system as a whole. Massive social change is compounded out of slight shifts in individual attitudes and beliefs.

From this point of view, higher education can be seen to have

[3] There are, of course, a number of relatively small institutions which turn out independent thinkers, radicals, and rebels with some regularity. Their graduates are likely to be students who possessed a predilection as freshmen for this kind of change. When they have a choice among colleges, students are likely to choose the one which will influence them in ways that are congenial to them. See McConnell, Thomas R., and Heist, Paul. The Diverse College Student Population. In Sanford, Nevitt (Ed.). *The American College.* New York: Wiley, 1962.

exerted a profound influence on American life and society, notably since the Depression years and especially since World War II. Generations of students have emerged from commencement exercises with a greater commitment to the liberal view than they had at the time of college entrance. By "liberal view," I mean appreciation of the complexity of people and social events, openness to new experience, flexibility in thinking, compassion in judgment of people, and the like. These changes are large in some students, small in others. But few go through college these days without acquiring at least a tinge of this liberalization. And the social consequences of such changes are enormous.

What is happening now is that administrators and faculty members are being overwhelmed by their very success in liberalizing students. To a considerable extent the student unrest of the last several years, which has taken so many administrators and faculty members by surprise, is a reflection of the degree to which liberal education has taken hold. The students have taken the rhetoric of liberal education seriously. The faculty members and administrators, on the other hand, have regarded statements about the glories of liberal education in the same way that most American citizens lend an ear to Fourth of July oratory.

The way in which large-scale social events and social movements may be based on slight shifts of attitude among individuals is illustrated by the way that a city like Atlanta, Georgia, has integrated public facilities in recent years with relatively little difficulty. Surely, as various public-opinion surveys show, this is not the result of any major change in outlook among its individual white citizens. The majority of them would prefer that segregation be maintained. They do not regard Negroes as equals now any more than they did ten years ago, and they do not care to share public life with them. What has changed is the vehemence with which such views are held. A white citizen of Atlanta will now accept, albeit grudgingly, a condition that he would have forcibly resisted some years ago.

One may account for national differences in culture and politics in similar fashion. Consider the question of why the German people fell victim to Hitler and his Nazi police state. It would seem that a certain authoritarian disposition in the personality structure of Germans, at least many of them, is surely part of the explanation. Yet when one meets Germans, or spends some time in Germany, individuals seem to differ little from citizens of other countries. As far as authoritarian qualities are concerned, Germans seem to exhibit a considerable range. There is only a slight tendency for Germans to be more authoritarian than Americans or Frenchmen. At the level of dealing with individuals this tendency is barely noticeable. But its summation over many hundreds of thousands of people can result in acquiescence to a thoroughgoing police state.

I came to appreciate these processes of social change in the course of studying the attitudes and opinions of Vassar alumnae of various decades.[4] During 1957 and 1958 I administered the California Public Opinion Survey[5] to groups from the classes of 1904, 1914, 1920–22, 1929–35, 1940–42, and 1954. Contrary to my expectations, I discovered that there were many and significant differences in response between women of adjacent decades. I had presumed that experiences during the years after graduation would influence alumnae in ways such that women who were reasonably close in age would hold rather similar views on political, social, and economic issues.

So, for example, I had anticipated that the responses of the alumnae of the classes of 1904 and 1914 would look much alike. At the time the questionnaires were administered, these women's ages averaged seventy-four and sixty-six years respectively. They had shared the experiences of World War I, the Jazz Age, the Depression, World War II, the Korean War, the McCarthy era, and the Eisenhower Administration. Surely any original differences between these groups that might have existed at the time of graduation from Vassar would have been obliterated by the influence of the intervening years. It developed, however, that the women in these two groups were rather far apart on a number of issues. Moreover, the differences seemed to reflect the ethos of the times

[4] See Chapter 6.

[5] The California Public Opinion Survey contains measures of Authoritarianism, Ethnocentrism, and Political Economic Conservatism. (See Chapter 6 for a description of these scales.)

at which they had been in college—the progressive era of Woodrow Wilson, for example, versus the more conservative period of William McKinley. It appeared that the attitudes one has toward political, social, and economic issues at the time one leaves college have remarkable persistence. Other studies have supported this finding.[6]

So it is that higher education has come to exert a profound influence on American life. Liberal education affects some students appreciably and "rubs off" on many thousands more, and these changes in individuals ramify throughout American society and culture. Moreover, the proportions of youth who attend college are increasing at a considerable rate.[7] We may, therefore, presume that the social consequences of college attendance will be greatly magnified.

A recently published book[8] contends that most personality and intellectual characteristics are laid down in infancy and early childhood and that they are extremely resistant to later change, even in primary school years. For example, from ages eight to seventeen the most radical change in environment produces an average change of only 0.4 IQ points per year—a difference of four IQ points in ten years. The midpoint on the scale of development of characteristics such as intelligence, academic achievement, and aggression comes before age five. For Bruno Bettelheim, this is evidence that significant change in behavior and personality cannot take place in school.[9]

[6] Bugelski, B. Richard, and Lester, Olive. Changes in Attitude in a Group of College Students during Their College Course and after Graduation. *Journal of Social Psychology,* 1940, **12,** 319–332; Nelson, Erland N. P. Persistence of Attitudes of College Students Fourteen Years Later. *Psychological Monographs,* 1954, **68** (Whole No. 373); Newcomb, Theodore M. *Personality and Social Change.* New York: Dryden, 1943.

[7] A. J. Jaffe and Walter Adams contest this commonly accepted view. They argue that the proportion of high school students who go on to college now does not differ from the proportion of a century ago. Increases in enrollment are a function of population expansion. See Jaffe, A. J., and Adams, Walter. Trends in College Enrollment. *College Board Review,* Winter 1964–65, **55,** 27–32.

[8] Bloom, Benjamin S. *Stability and Change in Human Characteristics.* New York: Wiley, 1964.

[9] Bettelheim, Bruno. How Much Can Man Change? Review of Bloom,

It is true that a net gain of four IQ points is not likely to make a discernible difference in the life of one person. Yet an average gain of four IQ points in hundreds of thousands of individuals may be of considerable social consequence. The process of biological evolution rests on such a basis—the emergence of minute physical and physiological changes that make it easier for the individual organism and the species to survive and prosper. Similarly, social and cultural change—for better or for worse—rests on parallel minute shifts in attitude and personality characteristics. On this basis we may account for the phenomena of Hitler and the Nazi movement and for the civil rights movement in the United States today. This is how very large numbers of people can be influenced to participate in such movements or at least to acquiesce to their principles.

Still, although I have stressed the beneficial social and cultural consequences of the effects of college attendance, my view is not one of unqualified optimism. I have on many occasions argued that American higher education hardly scratches the surface. Colleges and universities could contribute much more than they do to the personal development of students and to society at large.

Moreover, although the changes that occur in the personality during the college years tend to have considerable persistence, circumstances during the postcollege years can alter this situation. In recent decades the American political and social climate has favored the liberal position. The liberalizing influences of college experience have, therefore, been reinforced in the years after graduation. In 1936 Erland Nelson tested 3,758 college students on their political, social, and economic outlooks, and in 1950 he repeated the tests with 901 of his original subjects.[10] Nelson discovered that his subjects maintained their original positions with a considerable degree of consistency, but with a postcollege trend toward "slightly more liberalism." In the subsequent McCarthy era of the early 1950's, however, restrictive sentiment concerning the exercise of traditional American freedoms by Communist and other dissident

---

Benjamin S. *Stability and Change in Human Characteristics.* In *The New York Review of Books,* September 10, 1964, p. 3.

[10] Nelson. Persistence of Attitudes.

groups increased among college-educated citizens.[11] Gallup polls in that period show a significant rise in the proportion of college alumni who would deny various rights to people identified with Communist positions, even though these alumni were more liberal than citizens with less education. Apparently, strong pressures, such as those exercised by the forces of public opinion in support of Senator McCarthy, can bring about changes in beliefs and attitudes among college alumni. One may not, in short, be too sanguine about the personality changes that are wrought by liberal education. Often they are not significant alterations of personality structure but rather represent what Carl Bereiter has called "sophistication of attitude." Such changes are only superficial, and in the face of counter pressure, many alumni may revert to less liberal positions.

Surely, it is difficult to be hopeful about the results of higher education when one considers the personal and social demands of the future. Enormous effort and wisdom will be required simply to prevent a nuclear holocaust. The task of making viable communities out of big cities is hardly less formidable. One can easily compile a list of problems and social issues of almost equal magnitude. Colleges and universities have made important contributions to American society and culture, but the crucial test of their value lies ahead.

With each passing year, larger proportions of American youth will be matriculating in college. If they can be influenced in significant ways, they may well save the world. As Chapter 13 makes clear, I do not use these words in idle rhetoric. I believe that, if we get through the next decade without nuclear war, we shall see the beginnings of a much better world. Youth will bring this about, provided that our colleges and universities furnish adequate leadership. The message of this chapter is that it can be done. It requires, however, that the impact of college experience on the individual student be sharper and deeper than has been customary heretofore.

[11] Stouffer, Samuel A. *Communism, Conformity, and Civil Liberties.* Garden City, New York: Doubleday, 1955.

2

The College and the Image of Man[1]

William Blake, who lived from 1757 to 1827, had a vision—or rather, a series of visions. He recognized that Newton, Locke, and mechanistic science meant the end of the Christian myth. Blake

[1] At the time I outlined this book early in 1966, I did not plan to include this essay. It was written in 1963, when technical competition with Russia in the post-Sputnik spirit was still the order of the day, and early in 1966 its description of students and the college did not seem so accurate any longer. Student unrest subsequent to 1963 and the changes among faculty and administrators that I depict in Chapter 14 seemed to render my views less apposite.

The introduction of the College Qualification Test into the college scene in April 1966, however, has led me to include this chapter. The nightmare world of 1984 in which individual hopes, desires, and fulfillment are subordinated to the needs of the state once more becomes a tangible threat. In order to escape the draft a young man must now be registered in college; he must show evidence that he is not dallying on the way to a degree; and he must be winning out in the competition for grades with his peers. The words of Lady Ethel Venables become more appropriate: "A solemn meritocracy which undervalues the less able and leaves no room for gaiety and nonsense in the tidy plans will inevitably breed the rebellious young people it deserves." Proposed Affinities in British-American Perspectives of Adolescence. *Journal of Marriage and the Family,* 1965, **27**, 148–155.

saw the "Satanic wheels" and the "Satanic mills" of rising industry as symbols of an impersonal and inhuman society of constraint.

He envisioned the society of the future as characterized by increasing competition, struggle for worldly success, and suppression of the imagination and the instincts—a joyless life. He saw the universities contributing to this trend.

> I turn my eyes to the Schools and Universities
> of Europe
> And there behold the Loom of Locke, whose
> woof rages dire,
> Wash'd by the Water-Wheels of Newton: Black
> the cloth
> In heavy wreathes folds over every Nation. . . .[2]

Unhappily, Blake's predictions have been borne out. I quote Henry Murray:

> After Blake the rapid advance of science and industry, combined with the puritan ethic and buttressed by rationalism, produced within a century a moralistic-mechanistic culture which proved so oppressive to the erotic imagination, to all joyous originations in art, in religion, in life, that the suffering depths of the mind became a breeding ground of elemental resentments, of an all-embracing hostility, and in extreme cases, of nihilism . . .

Murray goes on to speak of developments after World War I:

> . . . finally [came] Mechos, the cold-blooded dragon of impersonal matter-of-factness and technics, of business, advertising, and upward mobility, of hollow showmen and spurious prestige; the machine-god that seemed to be getting grosser and more implacable every day and shaping more and more robots in its own image to propagate still more omnipotent machines.[3]

[2] Blake, William. A Vision of Albion. In Sampson, John (Ed.). *William Blake's Poetical Works*. London: Oxford University Press, 1913 (reprinted 1960), p. 388.

[3] Murray, Henry A. Conrad Aiken: Poet of Creative Dissolution. *Perspectives,* Fall 1953, No. 5, 28–29.

Prior to World War II, the great American colleges stood somewhat aloof from this state of affairs. There was time for taking football seriously. The leisurely life of the gentleman of an earlier day was still possible. The "gentleman's C" was still in vogue. The faculty participated little in the traffic of the market place. They had time for contemplation, for unhurried thought not tied to immediate outcome.

I do not wish to heap uncritical praise upon the colleges of an earlier day. There were many things wrong with them, and it could hardly be argued that the majority of their graduates were exemplars of liberal education. Nevertheless, prior to World War II, students and faculty members were not immersed in the mainstream of American life. They had much freedom in deciding what they would do and how they would do it.

All this has changed. College attendance has become an integral part of the American way of life. The national purpose and college attendance coincide. An individual of above-average intelligence who chooses not to go to college may not be morally reprehensible, but he is certainly no patriot. Students are encouraged to work harder and harder at earlier and earlier ages to absorb the knowledge of various disciplines and to prepare for college, where they will work harder still. This hardheaded, no-nonsense view of education has produced some very strange bedfellows. Admiral Rickover may be found cheek by jowl with faculty deans; insurance agents who encourage clients to assume policies for the education of their sons and daughters with spokesmen for various learned societies; and right-wingers denouncing educational "frills" with people of a liberal political outlook.

Since World War II, the prominent colleges have participated increasingly in this ethos of college attendance, and the effects upon students have been devastating. With each passing year, students in these colleges seem more like Israelites groaning under the Egyptian's lash—humorless, leisureless, guilt-ridden drudges. They are harried on all sides by reading lists that are impossibly long and assignments that cannot be completed except by cutting corners. Knowledge in all fields is being produced at an explosive rate, and faculty members, bent on teaching their own disciplines, presume that each generation of undergraduates should absorb the steady increase of information. Competition among students is intensified every year by admitting a class that is somewhat better academically than the previous one, according to criteria such as secondary school grades or college-board scores. In short, successive freshman classes face progressively tougher competition from fellow students and greater demands from the faculty.

Demands for earlier and earlier professional commitment have also intensified. Programs such as summer workshops supported by government agencies and private foundations have helped this process. The faculties of various departments compete for the best students, whom they attempt to recruit as early as possible and to mold in the prevailing images of their respective fields. Despite obeisance to liberal education in catalogues and public pronouncements and the presence of interdisciplinary courses in the curriculum, the prominent colleges have become, since World War II, more and more exclusively training grounds for graduate and professional schools and for business.

What is disturbing about students is not that they submit to these demands—there is, after all, little else that they can do if they wish to go to a prominent college and remain there after they are admitted—but that so many have acquired a slave mentality. They are uncomfortable unless they are working hard or even being overworked. A faculty member who tries to counter these trends by assigning only light tasks, in the hope of encouraging students to think more deeply or broadly than they would in the press to fulfill lengthy requirements, may find his course termed "Mickey Mouse," or something equally contemptuous.

Yet what else can we expect of students who have been conditioned by years of social and family pressure to perform well academically? In middle-class neighborhoods, the pressure on schools to prepare students for the most outstanding colleges has descended to early primary school age groups. These students have lived for years with demands for high grades and hopes for high college-board scores.

We cannot be content with placing such demands on students unless we examine the goals that are served by these demands. If we require hard work and excellent performance in students we must ask: for what personal or social ends?

Nevitt Sanford has pointed out the hazards of defining excellence in too narrow a fashion.[4] In the middle classes, excellence is equated with academic and later business or professional success; and achievement of this kind is becoming the sole standard by which middle-class boys and girls and young men and women evaluate their own worth.[5] The only other path to recognition that is available to such young men is athletic prowess, but even this has declined in prestige.

Given the fierce competition fostered by the admissions requirements, grading systems, and other evaluative procedures in the prominent colleges, academic performance as the almost exclusive criterion of worth and self-respect seems very dubious indeed. There can be few A's and few top performers; most students are destined for B's and C's. Are students with mediocre grades to feel defeated, to feel they are worth little as human beings? Surely there are other standards by which young people who do not do well academically or who do not even go to college may judge themselves and be judged.

Not all students, of course, bow slavishly to stringent academic demands. A small number can function within the system and still rise above it. A somewhat larger number withdraw—at least temporarily—from the whole enterprise. They leave college to go to Europe to "hack around" for a year, or they go to work in a service station or an office at home. Other young men and women remain in college but otherwise withdraw as far as they can from its formal educational aspects; they enter into artistic enterprises, study mystical Eastern religion and philosophy, or experiment with drugs.[6] These young men and women who have worked very hard to gain

[4] Sanford, Nevitt. One Cheer for Excellence. In *The Intellectual Climate of the Liberal Arts Colleges*. Claremont, Calif.: The Claremont Colleges, 1963.

[5] Such pressures are, of course, greater in the case of men. Women have the option of "retreating" into marriage. These pressures on educated women are mounting, however.

[6] The draft, with its pressure for high grades, has made such a solution difficult if not impossible for most men.

admittance to a prominent college—and who then proceed to turn away from their former goals—are symptoms of disorder and obliquity.

Most students conform to the system. What is worse is that most faculty conform as well. It is often said that one of the prime functions of a college is to serve as a critic of society. After all, there has been in American intellectual life a deep stream of dissent running back to Emerson and Thoreau. Certain public officials, however, can try to mold the education of young men to suit national policy in a way that seems frighteningly totalitarian, and hardly a voice is raised in protest by the faculties and administrations of the prominent colleges.[7]

Colleges that demand more and more effort from youth, foster intense competition among them, and push them to choose their major field of study and define themselves vocationally and professionally earlier and earlier in life can lead only to the empty, joyless existence of Blake's vision. What is needed of our best-educated men and women is originality, not conformity. We need dissent, not compliance—reasoned dissent, not blind rebellion, but dissent nonetheless. As Jacob Bronowski has said, "No society is strong which does not acknowledge the protesting man."[8] American society and its prominent colleges have, since World War II, been marching together in a lockstep that has all but ruled out the possibility of producing the rational protesting man. If this educational trend prevails, the best that one can hope for is the preservation of the status quo in American society, with the addition of certain technical improvements.

Those individuals who consider the prime road to advancement of culture and knowledge to be unswerving application to

[7] Protests against the College Qualification Test by administrators and faculty members of a number of colleges are a recent and important exception. Such protests tend to be tied in with expression of considerable dubiety concerning American foreign policy (see Chapter 14). Considering the debilitating effects of the draft and the College Qualification Test on the opportunities for students to suspend commitment and to explore, essentials of liberal education, these expressions of disapproval seem very feeble. They have been confined to few institutions and to relatively few individuals. The great majority of American educators have been silent.

[8] Bronowski, J., *The Face of Violence*. New York: Braziller, 1955, p. 62.

study and competition among students might well ponder the circumstances of one of the most important scientific discoveries of all time, made by one of the most creative men who has ever lived. Isaac Newton's discovery of gravitation took place, as we all know, when Newton watched an apple fall from a tree. At the time he was sitting idly in his mother's garden. He was not at Cambridge because in that year, 1665, the plague broke out in southern England, and Cambridge was closed for eighteen months. We know from Newton's own account what his state of mind was at the time of his discovery. He described himself as being in an eager, boyish mood. "I was," he said, "in the prime of my age for invention."[9] How unlike the mood of most American college youth!

Similarly, we may ponder the low opinion of academic success held by the Yeats family, which produced the poet and dramatist, William Butler, and his brother, Jack Butler, the painter. When Jack was a boy and was at the bottom of his school class, his grandmother is reported to have commented, "Examinations are vulgar, trying to show that one boy is better than another. I'm glad our boy failed."[10] As matters stand now, a mediocre student like the young John Kennedy or Adlai Stevenson, who is to go a long way but who shows little academic sign of it in early life, would probably have a difficult time gaining admittance to a prominent college or remaining there if admitted.

Some may consider my judgments of the great American colleges to be unduly harsh. Blake's vision of a joyless life and an inhuman society of constraint may seem far removed from the campuses they know. In some of these colleges today, the cloud of narrowness and conformity may be no bigger than a man's hand; but given the swift pace of change in the dynamic American society, in a few years the sky could be darkened. Surely, there are no easy solutions to the state of affairs I have described. One thing, however, is certain: Instead of bowing facilely to the transient needs of American society, the leading colleges must exert pressures on that society in the direction of greater individual and social freedom.

[9] Newton, Isaac. As quoted in Bronowski, J. *Science and Human Values.* New York: Harper, 1959, p. 25.

[10] Atkinson, Brooks. Continuing Influence of W. B. and J. B. Yeats. *The New York Times,* December 14, 1962, p. 5.

II

PERSONALITY DEVELOPMENT IN THE COLLEGE AND ALUMNI YEARS

3

Personality Development in the College Years

At first glance, the phenomenon of development or change in students in college seems to defy analysis and generalization. How can one say anything that is cogent, systematic, and accurate about college attendance? Students are rich and poor; Catholic, Protestant, and Jewish; Negro, Caucasian, and Oriental; smart and not-so-smart (in fact, given the ubiquitousness of current college attendance, some students are even dumb). There are residential colleges, commuter colleges, prestigious colleges, and colleges so small as to be almost completely unknown outside their own localities. Some students queue up for the good life as represented by IBM, *Time, Life, Fortune,* and U.S. Steel; others grow beards and attend protest rallies. Some students marry; some even get divorces. Is there really an order to be found in this profusion of conditions and behavior? It often seems doubtful. But if one plunges in, sustained by Einstein's faith that "God does not play dice with the world," he is likely to be rewarded.

By "personality," I mean what an individual means when he says "I"—the whole person. Development in personality then includes changes in intellectual abilities and thinking; changes in opinions, beliefs, and values, that is, in what is often called character; and changes in internal psychological processes, for example, emotional stability versus instability, mechanisms of defense, and attitudes toward oneself and other people.

I shall concentrate here on changes in character and in other general features of personality.[1] Important changes in intellectual ability—in such characteristics as reasoning, memory, and judgment—do occur during this period, however, and this is an important point. It is generally assumed that after age sixteen or seventeen increase in mental abilities is negligible. Many of the activities of college selection, application, and admission are based on this belief. This view is an oversimplification. Evidence is increasing[2] that there are large individual differences in the time of life at which maximum mental ability is attained. A study by Nancy Bayley and Melita Oden[3] demonstrated that gifted adults made substantial gains in reasoning ability even after age thirty. It appears that the more intelligent subjects of any particular age, in comparison with less intelligent people of the same age, are not only increasing in measured ability at a faster rate, but also are farther both in time and in amount from their point of maximum ability.[4] Increases in mental ability may therefore be anticipated among many students after they enter college, and marked increases have been observed for some students.[5] The chances are that improvement of intelli-

[1] I should like to make it clear that I consider this separation of intellectual or cognitive functioning from other processes of the personality to be a very artificial procedure. People operate as wholes. Changes in one part of the total system influence all other parts. So it is that one should not—really cannot—do what is so often done, that is, to treat intellectual or cognitive processes as if they were fixed entities, independent of other aspects of human functioning.

[2] Bayley, Nancy. Data on the Growth of Intelligence between 16 and 21 Years as Measured by the Wechsler-Bellevue Scale. *Journal of Genetic Psychology,* 1957, **90,** 3–15.

[3] Bayley, Nancy, and Oden, Melita. The Maintenance of Intellectual Ability in Gifted Adults. *Journal of Gerontology,* 1955, **10,** 91–107.

[4] Bayley, Nancy. Individual Patterns of Development. *Child Development,* 1956, **27,** 45–75.

[5] Florence, Louise M. Mental Growth and Development at the College

gence tests will reveal even more change in ability, both in degree and in kind, among future college students.

Many educators and administrators are bothered by changes in intellectual functioning during the college years. They want to categorize students along axes of ability, so that colleges and universities may be compared one with another or students referred to the college appropriate to their abilities. Fluctuations in score which appear to represent true change rather than error of measurement get in the way of these sorting and categorizing enterprises. In these days of bigness and bureaucracy, however, it is encouraging to know that some individuals will not stand still to make it easy for an official of one kind or another to reduce them to fixed statistics. The development of the individual to the fullest extent possible is, of course, the most appropriate educational goal in a democracy, and it is salutary to realize that even intellectual ability, which has long been regarded as a stable property or characteristic in adulthood, cannot be assumed to be fixed by the time of college entrance.

The possibility of effecting significant change in personality is, of course, the faith upon which liberal education is based. If one asks a group of liberal educators what it is they are trying to do to or for students, the answer sometimes comes back as simply "the training of the mind." Sometimes cognitive or intellectual goals are conceived more broadly as the "imparting of skills and information" or "knowledge of our cultural heritage." More often than not, however, the ends of education are defined by liberal educators in unequivocal terms of character or personality. Consider such expressed goals as "less prejudice in thinking, greater self-awareness, better understanding of other people and other cultures, or increased social responsibility." The catalogues of liberal arts colleges abound in statements of this kind, which presume implicitly that col-

---

Level. *Journal of Educational Psychology,* 1947, **38,** 65–82; McConnell, Thomas R. Changes in Scores on the Psychological Examination of the American Council on Education from the Freshman to the Senior Year. *Journal of Educational Psychology,* 1934, **25,** 66–69; Silvey, Herbert M. Changes in Test Scores after Two Years in College. *Educational and Psychological Measurement,* 1951, **11,** 494–502.

leges are capable of bringing about such character or personality changes in students.

In his essay "The Aims of Education," Alfred North Whitehead writes:

> Culture is activity of thought, and receptiveness to beauty and humane feeling. Scraps of information have nothing to do with it. A merely well-informed man is the most useless bore on God's earth. What we should aim at producing is men who possess both culture and expert knowledge in some special direction. . . . We have to remember that the valuable intellectual development is self-development, and that it mostly takes place between the ages of sixteen and thirty.[6]

By contrast, until very recently, psychiatrists, psychoanalysts, and psychologists have tended to emphasize the fixity of the personality in the college years. Most psychologists who are interested in cognitive and intellectual development have regarded mental ability as relatively fixed by about age sixteen. Those in the psychodynamic tradition have regarded the years of early adolescence, the years eleven or twelve to perhaps sixteen, as the last period in which important personality change takes place normally or spontaneously. Many writings in psychiatry, psychoanalysis, and psychology seem to suggest that there are two kinds of college students: those who are normal and ready to be educated, and those who are neurotic and need psychotherapy as well as education.

This traditional view of personality development in the college years comes from assigning overweening importance to the events of infancy and early childhood. According to this view, the really important things occur in the first five or six years of life. At puberty there is a resurgence of some of the conflicts of childhood. But by about age sixteen, the personality is fairly well shaped. Short of a psychoanalysis or other deep-going psychotherapy, nothing is likely to change it appreciably. A reading of Sigmund Freud's works shows that, in almost every case, the crucial events are seen

[6] Whitehead, Alfred North. *The Aims of Education and Other Essays*, New York: Mentor, 1949, p. 13.

to occur very early in life. The most noteworthy exception I could find was the case of a young woman who, according to Freud, "In childhood . . . had passed through the normal attitude characteristic of the feminine Oedipus complex," but who in adolescence became homosexual. Freud goes on to say: "The event which is so significant for our understanding of the case was a new pregnancy of her mother's and the birth of a third brother when she was about sixteen." Thus he states: ". . . we might . . . be inclined to classify the case as one of late acquired inversion."[7] Explanations of the etiology of personality disorder which employ this principle of late acquisition are rare indeed in Freud's works, however, and in the writings of other psychoanalysts as well.

I am not arguing that events of childhood are not important to the adult personality. Personality is of a piece throughout a lifetime, and obviously a college student is very much a product of his earlier experiences. I do object, however, to the view that psychoanalysis or similar procedures provide the only way in which important personality change may take place. The situation of the college student, particularly that of the freshman, would appear to be highly favorable to change. His social role of learner is defined to a considerable extent in terms of readiness to change, and his life circumstances are marked by the relative absence of commitments and encumbrances. Matriculation at almost any college is likely to offer students a high degree of independence compared with previous home and school situations. Given these conditions, some change seems to be almost inevitable, and I believe that small initial changes can ramify throughout the system and effect significant changes in the whole personality. One or several courses, a friendship with a fellow student, reading the poems of Keats or Wordsworth (we know from his autobiography that John Stuart Mill believed that poetry had saved him from madness), or a relationship with a faculty member can alter the personality in dramatic ways, initiating changes that may persist over a lifetime.

Very important changes in personality can and often do take

[7] Freud, Sigmund. The Psychogenesis of a Case of Homosexuality in a Woman. In Jones, Ernest (Ed.). *Collected Papers.* London: Hogarth, 1950, Vol. 2, pp. 211, 213, 226.

place spontaneously during the college years. By "spontaneously," I mean in the absence of planned intervention into the lives of individual students, such as psychotherapy. Students themselves tend to be of two minds about the prospect of change. On the one hand, they have great expectations and fantastic hopes of what college may do for them. I say "fantastic" because various studies[8] have demonstrated that the deepest fantasies of young people, fantasies of romance or of extraordinary achievement, tend to be stirred when they think of college. On the other hand, however, students tend to have little confidence in their own ability to bring about these marvelous changes. They adopt a passive attitude and look hopefully to something outside themselves, to the vague entity known as "the college," which they hope will somehow accomplish the great things they would so much like to see happen.

It is this lack of confidence in their own potential for development that allows the essential tragedy of college attendance to occur. I refer to the tragedy of freshmen becoming upperclassmen or graduating seniors. Anyone who observes a class of freshmen during orientation week must be enormously impressed by their spirit, their idealism. The chances are that the very same group of students will look quite different a few years later. They will have become hardened; they will have become indistinguishable from the rest of us prosaic adults. What has happened, of course, is that these students have been socialized by the college. They have been initiated into the ranks of college students and college alumni. The demands of these roles will have taken precedence over the kinds of development that would have had far more intrinsic meaning and worth for the individual student. Were entering freshmen to have somewhat greater confidence in their own potential to bring about the fantasied prospects before them, this kind of mass socialization would not occur in quite so routine a fashion.

This kind of anonymous socialization would be tragic under any circumstances. But if we reflect on the future conditions of our

[8] Douvan, Elizabeth, and Kaye, Carol. Motivational Factors in College Entrance. In Sanford (Ed.). *The American College.*

society, we must recognize that about all we can be sure of in planning for them now is their unpredictability. The kinds of change in human existence that, in the past, evolved slowly over centuries are now compressed into generations or even decades. Professions and ways of life for which college students are now being prepared may become obsolete before students even enter them. The philosopher J. Bronowski says of the physical universe: ". . . the passage of time in the universe at large is marked by an increasing state of physical disorder or randomness . . . [so that] the future differs from the present by being statistically more random."[9] The uncertainty and unpredictability that characterize the physical universe are likely to be equally true of the human and social universe. The swift pace of change which characterizes western society demands that students and adults recognize their own potential for important personality change and struggle to maintain their flexibility.

As I have indicated, my remarks about the dulling effects of socialization in college should not be interpreted to mean that no personality changes of consequence occur during the college years. Empirical study of students demonstrates that important kinds of development in personality do occur.

The foremost is an increase in independence. At Vassar College, under the auspices of the Mary Conover Mellon Foundation, a number of colleagues and I carried out research on personality development in college. As a part of this research, Harold Webster developed the Developmental Status Scale,[10] which was based on analysis of all the items[11] which discriminated seniors from fresh-

[9] Bronowski, J., *The Common Sense of Science.* New York: Random House, 1955, p. 118.

[10] Webster, Harold. Changes in Attitude during College. *Journal of Educational Psychology,* 1958, **49,** 109–117.

[11] The basic item pool, in addition to items written by members of the staff of the Mellon Foundation, consisted of items drawn from the California Psychological Inventory (Gough, Harrison G. *Manual for the California Psychological Inventory.* Palo Alto, California: Consulting Psychologists Press, 1957), the Minnesota Multiphasic Personality Inventory (Hathaway, Starke, and McKinley, J. Charnley. *Manual for the Minnesota Multiphasic Personality Inventory* [Rev. Ed.]. New York: The Psychological Corporation, 1951), and the Maslow Test for Dominance Feeling in Women (Maslow, Abraham

men. The following are a sample of the 123 items which comprise the scale, the answers given being those that predominate among the seniors: "I have often gone against my parents' wishes" (true); "I set a high standard for myself and feel that others should do the same" (false); "It is annoying to listen to a lecturer who cannot seem to make up his mind about what he really believes" (false); "I would be uncomfortable if I accidentally went to a formal party in street clothes" (false); "It is a pretty callous person who does not feel love and gratitude toward his parents" (false); "I believe in a life hereafter" (false).

The general content of the items was classified under the following rubrics: freedom from compulsiveness, flexibility and tolerance for ambiguity, impunitive attitudes toward people in general, critical attitudes toward authority (including parents or family, the state, organized religion, rules, and the like), intraception (that is, "the dominance of feelings, fantasies, speculations, and aspirations —an imaginative, subjective human outlook"),[12] mature interests, unconventionality or nonconformity, rejection of traditional feminine roles, freedom from cynicism toward people, and realism. Outstanding among these varied traits were critical attitudes toward authority. Webster accordingly called the general factor which most clearly distinguished Vassar seniors from freshmen "rebellious independence." At the Center for the Study of Higher Education of the University of California at Berkeley, Paul Heist, T. R. McConnell, and Harold Webster have discovered that the Developmental Status Scale discriminates seniors from freshmen at other colleges as well. Further, the results hold for men as well as for women. Apparently an increase in "rebellious independence" is a widespread phenomenon in the college years.

Another scale which discriminates seniors from freshmen at Vassar and other colleges is the Impulse Expression Scale.[13] A sam-

---

H. Self-Esteem (Dominance Feeling) and Sexuality in Women. *Journal of Social Psychology,* 1942, **16,** 259–294). The Maslow items were reworded so as to be amenable to presentation in "true-false" form.

[12] Murray, Henry A. *Explorations in Personality.* New York: Oxford, 1938, p. 148.

[13] Sanford, Nevitt, Webster, Harold, and Freedman, Mervin. Impulse

ple of the 124 items which comprise the scale follows (again the responses are those characteristic of the seniors): "I enjoy discarding the old and accepting the new" (true); "I like dramatics" (true); "I often act on the spur of the moment without stopping to think" (true); "I like to flirt" (true); "I have never done anything dangerous for the thrill of it" (false). High scorers, or seniors, are dominant, aggressive, autonomous, and exhibitionistic, and they express interest in sex, excitement, and change.

Seniors also score significantly lower than freshmen on measures of authoritarianism. Authoritarianism is a personality syndrome which has yet to be defined with precision. It is nevertheless predictive of behavior in a variety of situations. Among many traits which are considered to be expressions of an authoritarian tendency are compulsiveness, rigidity, intolerance of ambiguity, punitive morality, submission to power, conventionality, cynicism, and anti-intraception. One measure of authoritarianism is the F Scale which was developed at the University of California.[14] This scale contains expressions of social attitudes and ideology: for example, "Science has its place, but there are many important things that can never possibly be understood by the human mind," or "What this country needs most, more than laws and political programs, is a few courageous, tireless, devoted leaders in whom the people can put their faith."

At Vassar College my colleagues and I developed another measure of authoritarian tendency which we called the Social Maturity Scale.[15] It correlates substantially (about —.75) with the F Scale in samples of college students. Unlike the items of the F Scale, the items of the Social Maturity Scale have a minimum of ideological content. Among the 149 items which comprise the scale are the following (the responses are those of the seniors, who display less

---

Expression as a Variable of Personality. *Psychological Monographs,* 1957, **72,** (Whole No. 440).

[14] Adorno, Theodor W., Frenkel-Brunswik, Else, Levinson, Daniel J., and Sanford, Nevitt. *The Authoritarian Personality.* New York: Harper, 1950.

[15] Webster, Harold, Sanford, Nevitt, and Freedman, Mervin. A New Instrument for Studying Authoritarianism in Personality. *Journal of Psychology,* 1955, **40,** 73–84.

authoritarian tendency): "Once I have my mind made up I seldom change it" (false); "Our thinking would be a lot better off if we would just forget about words like 'probably,' 'approximately,' and 'perhaps'" (false); "Parents are much too easy on their children nowadays" (false); "Most people make friends because friends are likely to be useful to them" (false); "A person does not need to worry about other people if only he looks after himself" (false).

The interpretation of these test findings is by no means simple. Do they represent true personality change? Or are they more superficial phenomena, indications of an awareness of the accepted thing to say or believe—a tendency which Carl Bereiter has called "increased sophistication of attitude"? Research that Bereiter and I carried out at Vassar suggested that both explanations are appropriate.

These test results and corroborative information obtained in other ways, for example, by means of questionnaires, interviews, and observation, also indicate that systematic personality change does occur during the college years. Development in this period is not simply a matter of progression along lines laid down in early adolescence or in infancy. Late adolescence, if we may bestow this label on the college years, is a period deserving attention in its own right, not simply a screen through which prior and more potent forces are filtered. It is a developmental phase with certain characteristic problems or conflicts and certain systematic ways of meeting them. Late adolescence may well prove to be as important for the adult personality as the developmental phases of infancy and early adolescence.

The chronology of the personality changes during the college years is an interesting phenomenon. The evidence is that the changes occur early, mainly within the first two years and particularly within the first year.[16] Moreover, these changes tend to last. When alumni who have been tested as seniors are retested five to fifteen years after graduation, results look quite similar. There is no evidence, for example, of a general tendency to revert to freshman

[16] Webster, Harold, Freedman, Mervin, and Heist, Paul. Personality Changes in College Students. In Sanford (Ed.). *The American College.*

norms or responses.[17] These findings suggest that we may think of a developmental phase of late adolescence as beginning at some point in secondary school and as coming to an end (at least for many students) by the end of the sophomore year of college. The fact that juniors and seniors may be in a developmental phase different from that of freshmen and sophomores may well be an argument for different kinds of college experiences for lower- and upperclassmen. In this sense, there may be a good deal of wisdom in the junior-college arrangement.

We are touching here on a very important point. Aside from instruction in certain kinds of skills and aside from occupational or professional training, the primary pressure of college education is in the direction described earlier—an increase in sophistication, complexity, relativism of outlook, and the like. When freshmen are unsophisticated, constricted, and undeveloped, as most of them still are these days, it is not too difficult to assess the effects of college attendance on the personality and to describe what it is that colleges may contribute to the development of youth. But what of the freshman who is already complex, sophisticated, critical of authority, and aware of his impulses? It is not so easy to know how the college experience will influence him. And given the tendency in American society for young people to mature at earlier and earlier ages (in the sense of becoming like people in the status or age groups next in line), there will be increasingly large numbers of freshmen in the future who are like upperclassmen in the colleges now.

I am currently involved in studies of students who, as freshmen, were more advanced developmentally than their fellow freshmen. It is my impression that these students often have rather a difficult time in college these days. They are vaguely or acutely dissatisfied. Outside of the acquisition of information, they feel that nothing much is happening to them; and I am inclined to agree. Many of these students drop out of college, either permanently or temporarily.

Until about a year ago, I was very perplexed and troubled by

[17] Freedman, Mervin. Studies of College Alumni. In Sanford (Ed.). *The American College.*

this phenomenon. It seemed to me that these students needed some kind of synthesis or unity in their lives. They needed a commitment or commitments, and it was not clear where such synthesis or commitment was to come from. Surely not from members of college faculties or from college administrators who seemed increasingly bent on sacrificing liberal education on the altar of sterile post-Sputnik technical competition with Russia or China. Nor from some abstract philosophy of the pursuit of excellence. As Nevitt Sanford has pointed out, all too often excellence means simply success within the existing system.[18]

I had not been one of those observers of college students who saw disorder, abandon, and crisis everywhere in their lives.[19] I had, in fact, argued the opposite—that most college students were too stable and complacent and needed to be stirred up a bit. Further, there was evidence[20] that students who utilized psychiatric services differed systematically from their fellow students who did not see themselves as in need of psychotherapy or psychiatric aid; it was likely that psychiatrists, psychoanalysts, and clinical psychologists had been generalizing about students on the basis of biased samples. There was no reason to think that neurosis or psychosis was proliferating on college campuses. Yet if the alternative to complacency and anonymous socialization was likely to be discouragement and alienation, the outlook in either case was rather grim. I could not see a really viable alternative to a large body of conventional, underdeveloped, half-educated students and a small but growing number of sophisticated and complex, but uncommitted and alienated, students.

Now, however, I see glimmers of hope. Interest in the liberal education of undergraduates is undergoing a revivification. In the near future, we may see a considerable swing away from the educational ethos which has made of many of our leading colleges and even secondary schools competitive pressure cookers in which stu-

[18] Sanford, Nevitt. One Cheer for Excellence.

[19] See Chapter 4.

[20] Webster, Harold. Some Quantitative Results. In Sanford, Nevitt (Ed.). Personality Development during the College Years. *Journal of Social Issues,* 1956, **12,** 29–43.

dents must devote a major share of their energies to vying with one another for future places in graduate and professional schools. I am convinced that in the next few years faculty members and administrators of many colleges will display a vigorous interest in the development of personality and character in students—in short, a vigorous interest in true liberal education.

Likewise, students themselves are beginning to display lively involvement in their own education. On a number of college campuses, students have organized themselves into groups or committees for the purpose of examining the curriculum or of meeting with faculty members and administrators in order to discuss educational issues. These activities are different from the traditional affairs of student government. They differ also from the customary behavior of students, which has been to accept passively whatever the college authorities meted out or, if the edicts of authority encroached too sharply on student autonomy, to react with blind rebellion.

Students, it seems, are trying to restore to colleges and universities the sense of community that has somehow been lost on most campuses since World War II. Before the war, college students shared certain things. They often were not academic experiences, but rather things like football games or fraternity life; still, they provided students with a feeling of belonging and participation. Academic culture has made sharp inroads into the student life of fraternities and sports. Academic and intellectual performance has been elevated, of course, but often at the expense of elements of life which students, being human, find it difficult to do without.[21]

Consider the situation of an entering freshman at a prominent college. He enters a complex social environment in which he knows few people. He feels very much on trial. He is unsure of himself and his abilities. Faculty members and administrators are likely to be perceived as distant and impartial judges. He may have been his class valedictorian in secondary school, but the quality of competition being what it is at most major colleges these days, he is likely to be a B student in his first quarter or semester. For someone ac-

[21] Sanford, Nevitt. Conclusions and Proposals for Change. In Sanford, Nevitt (Ed.). *College and Character.* New York: Wiley, 1964.

customed to straight A's, a B average can be a blow. Since he is in competition for grades with his fellow students, it is difficult to establish relationships with them in which he can relax and simply be himself. Of course, most students eventually recognize that they can perform at least adequately within the system. They do form friendships which provide mutual support and comfort. But even when this does occur, it is, as I have indicated, all too often a matter of anonymous socialization at the expense of intrinsic individual development.

Many students do not even arrive at the stage of community which I have called "anonymous socialization." My colleagues Elizabeth Alfert and Robert Suczek are engaged in studies of students who have dropped out of a large state university in their freshman or sophomore years.[22] One finding has been that the great majority of these students have not dropped out of school completely; they have transferred to other colleges, in most cases colleges smaller and closer to their homes. On questionnaires, these students indicate that they are happier after the transfer, and they complain about the loneliness of life at the university. Most of these dropouts are not cases of withdrawal because of academic failure.

Students are attempting to counter the atmosphere of competitiveness and isolation which has prevailed on our college campuses since the early 1950's. I believe they envision a community which encompasses much more than the traditional student society and culture that merely provided students with weapons for limiting the power and demands of faculty and administration or indoctrinated students in how to beat the system without running afoul of it.[23] What they have in mind, I believe, is a community which enables the individuals in it to develop themselves to the fullest degree possible. This means that many students are ready to appraise themselves and their social state with the expectation that

[22] Suczek, Robert, and Alfert, Elizabeth. Personality Characteristics of College Dropouts. Washington, D.C.: Educational Research Information Center, 1966.

[23] Becker, Howard, Geer, Blanche, Hughes, Everett C., and Strauss, Anselm L. *Boys in White,* Chicago: University of Chicago Press, 1961.

increased understanding will give them greater control over their institutional situation and their own development. They will have support from some members of the faculty and administration in this enterprise.

By examining what students are like now, one may glimpse the future of American society and culture. Arnold Toynbee thinks of the latter half of this century as an era of social reconciliation.[24] In religion, ecumenical movements will bring divergent groups together; in politics, the United Nations will fashion one world out of our currently diverse states. In my view, these massive social trends will be paralleled by developments at the level of smaller social units and even within the individual. I have referred to the restoration of the college as a viable social community. In industrialized, mobile America, communities as places in which people have strong personal ties to one another hardly exist. Such communities will have to be revived on a very widespread scale, however, if American society is to be rescued from submersion in alienation and anomie. Students are making a start at restoring a sense of community in the colleges, and they will, I believe, carry over their efforts to their social situation after college.

The Industrial Revolution introduced the practice of diversification of labor and knowledge. As the United States became rapidly industrialized in the decades after the Civil War, the college curriculum became increasingly fragmented. Major fields of specialization, departments, and divisions replaced a uniform curriculum and courses which emphasized synthesis in their approach to subject matter. This tendency reached its height in the post-Sputnik era. Now college students are beginning to reverse this trend. They are seeking greater breadth and unity of knowledge.[25] Specialized knowledge, what Whitehead called "expert knowledge in some special direction," will not disappear at the undergraduate level. But I do believe that students are attempting, by majoring in broadly defined fields of knowledge, to introduce a greater measure of

[24] Toynbee, Arnold. It is "One World or No World." *The New York Times Magazine,* April 5, 1964, 28–36.
[25] See Chapter 13.

wholeness or unity into their studies, their personalities, and their lives.

Given the perplexities and complexities of the future, college attendance must stand for more, and it must do more than it now does for students. The readiness for change is there, but the ability of students to bring about these changes is, of course, limited. Students cannot make the future on their own. They need leadership—leadership from educators and others who bear responsibility for the development of youth.

To provide such leadership is not a simple matter. Students want direction from adults, but as their need for autonomy burgeons during the college years, they are driven to reject adult leadership. Surely there is a great deal that adults cannot teach youth. To a considerable extent each generation must work things out on its own. This axiom becomes more true as western society becomes more and more complex.

Perhaps the most valuable way in which educators can contribute to the development of college students at this time is to reinforce their openness and readiness to change. In the face of uncertainty and confusion, students are often tempted to make commitments and decisions which they hope will resolve matters, but which are premature. So it is that sometimes they settle on careers or enter into marriages which are not appropriate for them and which they later regret.

The increasing complexity of western society demands that young people take a long time to develop and to find themselves. The period of life to be devoted to the state of student or the role of seeker or learner will be extended.[26] I believe, in fact, that activities of self-examination and social examination and of individual and social experimentation will become increasingly important throughout the whole life span.

As we have seen in the case of intellectual development, those individuals who are going far often take a long time to get there. If educators can help young people to tolerate uncertainty, am-

[26] See Chapter 13.

biguity, and confusion in their quest for self-development, I believe that they will be contributing immeasurably to the fullness of life for each individual student and to the ultimate enrichment and betterment of American society.

4

The Problem of Identity

Adolescence, according to most texts, is a time of psychological and social turmoil. The conflicts, urges, and anxieties of infancy and early childhood, which have been dormant in the latency period, are revived by the physiological changes of puberty and by new social demands. The adolescent displays inexplicable shifts of mood, is beset by doubt and guilt concerning sexual matters, rebels against parental standards, and so forth. Although a few writers have questioned the accuracy or current applicability of these observations,[1] it is generally accepted that "chronologically, adolescence may be viewed as beginning around thirteen-fourteen in a psychic dissolution, and terminating in a psychic consolidation at eighteen-twenty, with a mid-point at sixteen."[2] In this chapter, I shall review some

[1] Kuhlen, Raymond G. Adolescence. In Harris, Chester (Ed.). *Encyclopedia of Educational Research.* New York: Macmillan, 1960, pp. 24–30; Stone, L. Joseph, and Church, Joseph. *Childhood and Adolescence.* New York: Random House, 1957.

[2] Spiegel, Leo A. Comments on the Psychoanalytic Psychology of Adolescence. In *The Psychoanalytic Study of the Child.* New York: International Universities Press, 1958, p. 302.

of the results of a four-year program of interviewing college women, which suggest caution in generalizing from clinical populations to the whole range of adolescents. Studies of such normal samples—normal in the sense of not being patients—may well demonstrate that many of the views widely taken for granted have very shaky empirical foundations.

Of the college women interviewed, surprisingly few, less than one-third, had experienced or were then experiencing emotional or psychological difficulties of the kind regarded as routine among adolescents. The majority of subjects stated that early adolescence —that is, the years from about twelve to sixteen—had been reasonably placid, the difficulty most commonly reported having to do with acceptance by other girls; and while the college years for most of the subjects were more complex emotionally, only a minority appeared to be experiencing upheavals of an intensity sufficient to justify traditional views of adolescent turmoil.

The interviews were part of the long-range study of personality development in college women carried out at Vassar College under the auspices of the Mary Conover Mellon Foundation.[3] The observations reported here are based mainly on interviews with a random selection of one-fifth of a recently graduated class. These 80 subjects were interviewed periodically throughout their stay at the college, with the bulk of the interviewing taking place in the freshman and particularly the senior years. For the 47 subjects who remained in college until graduation and completed all of their interviews, the average number of interview hours was 20. Four other members of the sample were graduated with their class but did not complete all of the interviews—one because of outright resistance to the procedure, the other three because of problems of scheduling that probably stemmed from similar but less explicit opposition. The 29 students who withdrew from college prior to graduation were interviewed up to the time they left.

The interviews were semistructured. The interviewers were to

[3] Other aspects of this study have been reported elsewhere. Webster. Some Quantitative Results; Freedman, Mervin. Some Observations on Personality Development in College Women. Student Medicine, 1960, **8,** 228–245; Webster *et al.* Personality Changes in College Students.

obtain from each subject the information necessary to answer certain questions and to make certain ratings, but they were free to word questions as they saw fit or to pursue matters that seemed appropriate and important to personality development during the college years, even though these topics were not explicitly covered in the interview form. During the first three years the interviews were designed to last about one hour, but this was increased to one and one-half hours in the senior year. No attempt was made, however, to limit the length of interviews, and when there seemed to be good reason to delve deeply into the matters at hand and the student was disposed to do so, an interview could last for three or four hours. The interview staff consisted of four psychologists, a sociologist, and an anthropologist. Each student saw one of the staff members for most of her interviews, but not for all of them; in order to limit the development of transference phenomena or interviewer bias, interviews by two or three other staff members were interspersed during the four-year period.

The interviews were designed to elicit as comprehensive a picture as possible of the personality characteristics of the subjects and of their experiences during the college years. Among the topics covered were those that traditionally are of particular interest for psychoanalysis or dynamic psychology—for example, a description of family relationships; sources of happiness, satisfaction, fear, and anxiety; and a history of physical development. In addition, educational matters and values and attitudes were discussed.

Attitudes Toward Pubertal Changes and Sexual Matters

Of the 49 subjects from whom we obtained detailed histories of or attitudes toward the physiological changes of puberty and early adolescence, only five reported what seemed to be experiences of real strain or difficulty. When reminiscing on their feelings about such events as the onset of menarche or breast development, these five women made statements such as the following:

> It was a horror—one of the things you fear and conquer—I was relieved when it was over.

> It was definitely not welcome. I felt embarrassed and hated it.
>
> I had troubles. Mother was very Victorian and told me nothing. I learned a lot of things the wrong way. Eventually my older brother had to straighten me out.

A dozen other students indicated that the biological changes of puberty and early adolescence entailed some difficulty or stress, but not a great deal. The following remarks were typical of this group:

> I was a little embarrassed—also a little proud.
>
> Being a tomboy, I was embarrassed. I didn't want the boys to know.
>
> I was sort of annoyed by the cramps.
>
> It was scary although I knew all . . . the idea of becoming a woman.

The rest of the subjects reported that they were well prepared for the physical changes of puberty and that they accepted them rather matter of factly, or at least with a minimum of difficulty.

Knowledge about the biological changes of puberty and about sexual matters in general had been readily available to these students, and few had not received by the age of eleven or twelve at least the rudiments of sex education. In most cases some information had been supplied by a member of the family, usually the mother. Schools had also provided considerable instruction in these matters. And, of course, conversation with more knowledgeable girlfriends had been an important source of enlightenment.[4]

It may be argued, of course, that binding anxiety by means of intellectualizing defenses is the appropriate explanation for some of these results—that there is a considerable gap between possessing factual knowledge and being truly at home with it emotionally. This may well be, but whatever the reason, only a small minority of subjects reported the physiological changes of puberty to be a source of serious difficulty or disturbance.

If the relative placidity of puberty and early adolescence is

[4] There was one gap in knowledge of sexual matters—that of contraceptive techniques and devices. Even many seniors had little knowledge of this kind. See Chapter 8.

regarded as a defensive phenomenon of some kind, it is reasonable to hypothesize that problems centered on biological maturity and integration of sexual impulses were only postponed to some later period. Is there indication, then, of a fair degree of disturbance in sexual matters during the college years? The answer is no. The sexual behavior of most students was cautious or controlled. The majority were virgins at the time of graduation, and most of the students who had had sexual intercourse were seriously involved with or engaged to the men concerned. The number of students who might be described as promiscuous or even quite free was very small. Petting with rather definite limitations was the norm of sexual behavior. Few students seemed troubled by guilt feelings over their sexual activities. And few of those whose behavior was carefully controlled seemed to be seriously bothered by feelings of frustration. There were exceptions, of course, but it can hardly be said that sexual attitudes or activities during the college years constituted a major problem for most students.[5]

Rebelliousness toward the Family

Three students in the sample reported that the years from eleven to sixteen had been characterized by strong resentment of parental standards and by intense antagonism between themselves and other family members. Twelve others indicated that this period involved a moderate degree of rebellious feeling toward parents and some conflict with them. The remainder described surprisingly placid home lives. Resentment of parental regulations and family discord were not completely absent, of course, but the conflicts that arose were fairly readily resolved, usually by compromise of views on both sides. A parent who adhered rigidly to his own point of view, come hell or high water, was rare in this interview sample.

The quantitative studies[6] carried out at Vassar indicate that the expression of rebellious and critical attitudes toward parents increases during the college years. One measure of this increase was the Developmental Status Scale described in the preceding chapter.

[5] See Chapters 7 and 8.
[6] Webster. Changes in Attitude during College. See Chapter 3 also.

We will recall that "rebellious independence" toward authority and an attitude of tolerance toward human weakness differentiated college seniors from freshmen according to that scale. Needless to say, parents are among the authorities who are objects of this "rebellious independence." In addition, the questionnaires administered to freshmen and seniors contained a brief adjective checklist for indicating "the dominant attitude of your parents to you." Some of the adjectives were complimentary or favorable (for example, "generous" or "understanding"), while others connoted negative qualities (for example, "nagging" or "indifferent"). The number of unfavorable adjectives checked rose significantly between the freshman and senior years. And when the family-history interviews conducted in the freshman year were compared with those carried out in the senior year, it was apparent that most students had become more independent of family standards and that their attitudes toward their parents had grown more critical.

Nevertheless, these results cannot be interpreted to mean that the college years are, for the majority of students, characterized by crisis in relationships with parents. For the mosts part, the increases in critical and independent attitudes were absorbed into the personality with little stress. Of the 47 students who completed all the interviews, only 11 were judged to have experienced considerable conflict with parents during the college years. In very few cases, moreover, were such difficulties accompanied by marked symptoms or evidence of instability—inability to study with any degree of effectiveness, temporary withdrawal from school, or the like.

The quality of the process of emancipation from parents for most students is summed up in the following reply of a senior who was asked to describe the attitudes of her parents toward her college career: "They think I've been getting some ideas I shouldn't. I suppose that I have quietly drifted away from them quite a bit in many things. I can sense some disapproval at times, but they pretty much let me do what I think is right." And when asked to indicate the most important influence in her life, she said, "No matter how I may reject some things in my parents now, their ethics and standards have been very important."

General Stress and Instability

While the conflicts or difficulties considered so far have traditionally received most attention, others merit recognition. In recent years, for example, considerable interest has been focused on social problems, such as adolescent anxieties about dressing in the proper way and belonging to the right crowd. One might expect other sources of concern in, for example, a girl's relatively serious involvement with a boyfriend, problems connected with studies, and uncertainties about future careers.

The subjects were asked, during their senior year, "What have been the most stressful situations in your life?" The majority of respondents mentioned only one incident; few named more than two. The 49 replies that were readily classifiable break down as follows: family (divorce, arguments between parents, rejection by a parent, and the like), 13; boyfriends (rejection by a boy, parents' disapproval of a boyfriend, and so on), 13; social (not being in the right crowd of girls, feelings of shyness and awkwardness, and so on), 12; academic and career, 6; death or illness of a parent, 5.

It is striking that the physiological changes of puberty and early adolescence or directly sexual matters were not nominated even once, although three of the responses included in the category of "boyfriends" did involve some sexual conflict. Difficulties and strain within the family loomed large but by no means overshadowed problems with boyfriends and other girls. Furthermore, when the events of greatest stress were not chronic situations but could be assigned to a period of life—childhood, early adolescence, or the college years—the college years scored highest. Of the 31 situations that could be assigned to a specific point in time, 20 occurred during the college years, while only 11 took place earlier.

This is not to say, of course, that personal or familial difficulties during college may be regarded as independent of earlier events, except, perhaps, in such cases as the illness or death of a parent. Personality, after all, is of a piece throughout a lifetime, and events during the college years surely have prior origins. Nevertheless, the students in the interview sample considered puberty and early adolescence to have imposed less strain upon them than the college years.

These findings are in agreement with those reported by Elizabeth Douvan,[7] who has said: "I do think that in all likelihood feminine character develops later than masculine character, and that adolescence—the period we ordinarily consider par excellence the time for consolidation of character—is a more dramatic time for boys than for girls." In referring to early adolescence—that is, the years up to sixteen or so—Douvan states that girls are ". . . more likely to show an unquestioned identification with and acceptance of parental regulation. They less often distinguish parents' standards from their own—and they do not view the parents' rules as external or inhibiting as often as boys do."

The Minnesota Multiphasic Personality Inventory,[8] which was administered not only to the interview sample but also to the entire class in the freshman and senior years, provides an index of the degree of emotional difficulty experienced or the amount of pathological symptomatology displayed while in college. In keeping with the students' own views of the college years as entailing more emotional strain than earlier periods, there is some rise between the freshman and senior years on most of the clinical scales—for example, on the Hypochondriasis, Depression, Hysteria, Psychopathic Deviate, and Mania Scales. But although these differences between freshmen and seniors are significant for large samples, that is, for whole classes numbering several hundred students, they are small in magnitude. Only eight seniors—about one-sixth of the seniors in the interview sample—had profiles which might be regarded as abnormal.

Validity of the Interviews

The accuracy of information supplied by subjects in research of this nature is of crucial importance. Particularly when the inter-

[7] Douvan, Elizabeth. Character Process in Adolescence. Ann Arbor, Mich.: University of Michigan, 1957 (Dittoed).

[8] Hathaway, Starke R., and McKinley, J. Charnley. *The Minnesota Multiphasic Personality Inventory.* (Rev. Ed.) New York: The Psychological Corporation, 1951.

view deals with past events—for example, those occurring in early adolescence—it is often difficult to know what actually did happen. Conscious falsification was no real problem; most of the subjects became more interested and freer as the interviews progressed. But unconscious distortion must, of course, be reckoned with.

The standard theory of repression suggests that memories of past events have been altered in the direction of lessened conflict and strain. On the other hand, it is possible that ego growth during the college years decreases the need for distorting or repressive mechanisms, much as the strengthening of the ego in psychotherapy allows the recovery of repressed memories or permits seeing things in new ways. The increase in critical attitudes toward parents that occurs during the college years might be viewed in this light. Moreover, when members of the sample were interviewed in their senior year, they frequently described difficulty and stress that had occurred in the earlier college years but had not been reported at the time. The reasons for this were undoubtedly complex and may have included better rapport with the interviewers or enhanced insight from the perspective of several years of distance. But in my view the principal explanation is that growth in the ego had taken place. Being stronger, the students were better able to face facts about themselves.

Research on the validity and reliability of the anamnestic interview[9] indicates that the relationships between memories of past events and external judgments of these events are rather tenuous. These investigations do not, however, reveal a consistent tendency to view past events in a more favorable light. For example, the disposition to divest past events of the anxiety that was characteristic of them at the time of occurrence was found to be no stronger than the reverse tendency of attributing to these events, in memory, anxiety that was not reported at the time.[10] In short, there is no

[9] Haggard, Ernest A., Brekstad, Arne, and Skard, Aase Gruda. On the Reliability of the Anamnestic Interview. *Journal of Abnormal and Social Psychology,* 1960, **61,** 313–318; Pyles, M. K., Stoltz, H. R., and Macfarlane, Jean W. The Accuracy of Mothers' Reports on Birth and Development Data. *Child Development,* 1935, **6,** 165–176.

[10] See Haggard *et al.* On the Reliability of the Anamnestic Interview.

reason to think that the information supplied by the subjects in the interviews was subject to *systematic* alteration of any kind.

Distortions in Generalizing from Psychiatric Patients

In recent years the recommendation has been frequently made that workers in the psychological sciences pay greater attention to normal samples and to health and creativity, and some research of this nature has appeared.[11] But most of the literature dealing with general personality development is still based on knowledge gleaned from clinical practice. I am not arguing that study of disorder cannot reveal much about normal functioning. The whole history of the contributions of psychoanalysis to twentieth-century thought belies such a point of view. But generalizations based on observations of clinical populations can be misleading when applied indiscriminately to larger groups.

Much of the psychological and psychiatric literature dealing with college students is based on the 10 per cent or so of the student population who utilize counseling or psychiatric facilities. For example, the concept of "ego identity" has in recent years occupied a central place in interpreting the situation of the college student.[12] I do not object to the social emphasis introduced by the term. It has been salutary for theorists of adolescence or the college years to recognize that the problems and neuroses of these periods are not always primarily instinctual or biological in origin, and that they are not simply revivals of the Oedipus complex. It has been valuable to be reminded of the importance to adolescents of finding suitable places or roles for themselves in society.

[11] Murphy, Elizabeth, Silber, Earl, Coelho, George V., and Hamburg, David R. Development of Autonomy and Parent-Child Interaction in Late Adolescence. Washington, D.C.: National Institute of Mental Health, 1961; Raush, Harold L., and Sweet, Blanche. "The Preadolescent Ego: Some Observations of Normal Children." *Psychiatry,* 1961, **24,** 122–132; Westley, William A. Emotionally Healthy Adolescents and Their Family Background. In Galdston, Iago (Ed.). *The Family in Contemporary Society.* New York: International Universities Press, 1958; White, Robert W. *Lives in Progress.* New York: Dryden, 1952.

[12] Erikson, Erik H. "Identity and the Life Cycle." *Psychological Issues,* 1959, **1,** 1–171.

But I would question the emphasis on confusion and instability in the environment of college students. Helen Merrell Lynd, referring to the work of Erik Erikson, says: "He notes, in *Childhood and Society,* that because of the swift changes and dislocations of the contemporary world the search for identity has become as central in our time as the freeing of sexuality was in Freud's."[13] I doubt that such a description applies to many liberal arts college women. For example, consider the following two cases, young women who were studied by the Mellon Foundation at Vassar.

> Miss J., in the freshman interview that dealt with family life and general development prior to college entrance, could recall no stresses that amounted to anything. She was an only child, and while her parents had been devoted to her, they had established high standards for her and had held her to them. Although her parents had always expected much of her, she could not recall ever having rebelled seriously. Whenever differences arose, she and her mother could always reach some sort of agreement. Relationships between her parents always seemed to her to be excellent. She had been a somewhat better than average student all through school and had never experienced any noteworthy educational or academic problems. The family income was high, and she had not been troubled at any time by financial worries. As far back as she could remember she had got on well with other girls, had been reasonably popular with them, and had had a number of close girlfriends. Relationships with boys were similarly easy. She had started to go out with them on a limited basis at the age of thirteen, and her subsequent dates had involved a minimum of anxiety and difficulty. She reported no sexual problems. Although she indulged in some petting with boys of whom she was really fond, she set definite limits. She intended to remain a virgin until marriage, and she anticipated no difficulty in doing so.

One's first reaction to a report like this might be to conclude that massive repression or denial is at work. At any rate, this was

[13] Lynd, Helen M. Who are You? The Search for Identity in College. *Mademoiselle,* August 1960, 260–264.

my first response. According to Anna Freud, adolescence is by definition an interruption of peaceful growth.[14] In her opinion, those adolescents who do not display some form of upset are the victims of excessive defenses against their own drives, and are perhaps most in need of help to remove inner restrictions so as to allow normal maturation. This was a view that I shared, until longer acquaintance with this student and with others like her set me wondering. For as the weight of evidence of subsequent interviews and other observations of this young woman mounted, it became more and more difficult to dispute her view of things. To regard her as the victim of excessive defenses against drives was simply not appropriate. She was an average student, somewhat passive, rather conventional, and not very adventurous. But on the other hand, she had warmth and humor, and she was by no means closed to new experience. In short, at the end of the four-year interviewing program, my ideas about adolescent personality development had been shaken badly.

Four college years, of course, do not make a lifetime, and it may be that difficulties will manifest themselves at some future date. A study by the Mellon Foundation of college alumnae aged forty to forty-five showed that some women were experiencing severe emotional problems that had been too long postponed—problems that should have been dealt with at an earlier age.[15] Perhaps this will be the lot of Miss J. I did have the opportunity to interview her three years after her graduation, however, and at this time she seemed to be getting on very well. Married and the mother of two children, she seemed, if anything, to have grown in differentiation and complexity of personality.

Miss J., with her almost complete absence of emotional difficulties of any consequence, was by no means unique in the interview sample. Miss R. was a somewhat more complicated young

[14] Freud, Anna. *The Ego and the Mechanisms of Defense.* New York: International Universities Press, 1946; Adolescence. In *The Psychoanalytic Study of the Child.*

[15] Brown, Donald R. Some Educational Patterns. In Sanford (Ed.). Personality Development during the College Years; Freedman. Studies of College Alumni.

woman, whose life had not been so smooth as that of Miss J., but her adolescence and college years nevertheless did not warrant the label "crisis of ego identity."

> Miss R. reported a close and warm relationship with her mother but indicated that she had not really been close to her father. It had always seemed to her that he preferred her brother, who was two years younger, and she had resented this as far back as she could remember. She had been a tomboy in her girlhood and only reluctantly had given up boyish play and manners to assume the role of young lady in early adolescence. And, as one might expect, dating and friendships with boys had not come easily, When she was a freshman, Miss R. reported that she distrusted boys and did not feel at ease in their company. She became friendly with a young man in her sophomore year, however. As the relationship with him developed, her fear of intimacy with men gradually dissipated, and at graduation she was engaged to be married. Unlike Miss J., Miss R. was a brilliant student and intended to go on to graduate school. She planned to combine a scientific career with a family, anticipating that she would give up her work ouside the home when her children were young and resume it when they were old enough for her to be able to leave them during working hours.

Miss R. presents a picture that is apparently not without neurotic aspects. There seems to be evidence of some identification with her father as a frustrating object; at least her life history and her behavior in college display some phallic or traditionally masculine characteristics. And from all indications her choice of mate was that of a passive although reasonably competent fellow. Nevertheless, her difficulties or neuroses seemed to be maintained well within bounds. At graduation it appeared that she possessed the resources and organization required to live a reasonably adequate life by Freud's standards—that is, she was able to love and to work.

These cases were typical of about two-thirds of the subjects in the interview sample. Neurotic symptoms were conspicuous by their absence or were at least fairly well circumscribed. Moreover, when clearly observable symptomatology was present, it was reminiscent of the problems of Freud's day. That is, the neurotic problems were essentially variations of the classic one: How can the ego manage to include more of the impulse life in the face of the strictures of the superego? Such conflicts are probably less intense now than was the case in 1900, because today's less repressive culture and less authoritarian child-rearing practices permit the development of stronger egos and less rigid superegos.[16]

At any rate, I failed to see among the interview subjects a substantial number who would be classified as "problems of identity." Students troubled by the questions "Who am I?" and "Where do I fit in?" were not completely absent, but they comprised a distinct minority. It may be argued that the sample was very special, consisting as it did, of women of a special kind—primarily upper middle class, intelligent, highly motivated academically—in short, a superior and favored group. And it is true that things may be different for men. As I have mentioned, the research carried out by Douvan and her associates indicates that adolescence "is a more dramatic time for boys than for girls." But other studies suggest[17] that the Vassar-study results hold for a substantial number of women who attend liberal arts colleges.

The Stability of American Upper-Middle-Class Life

Even if the number of subjects about whom one can generalize is small, the sort of young women studied at Vassar comprise a group that possesses considerable social significance. For, as observers such as David Riesman[18] have pointed out, it is to the middle classes, and particularly to the upper middle class, that one must look for insights as to what the future offers. What holds for them now is likely to hold for larger segments of the population as time passes.

In view of the current situation of America's middle classes, it is not surprising that the majority of adolescents fail to display

[16] I believe that the popularization of psychology and psychoanalysis has profoundly influenced American middle-class family life in these ways.

[17] See Webster *et al.* Personality Changes in College Students.

[18] Riesman, David. Studies of Response to Social Change. *Journal of Social Issues,* 1961, **17,** 78–92.

a crisis of identity. At least among girls, the social scene seems to be characterized more by order and stability than by upheaval and dislocation. The pathways of life are clearly marked—school, college, marriage at a relatively early age, and children. In some cases a career is combined with marriage and children. Many of the old conflicts—for example, those of the feminist era between career and marriage—are now rather a thing of the past. To be sure, there are alternative ways of life, such as those of the beatnik or the dedicated artist who has neither time nor energy for anything other than her art, but these have few adherents. In a recent poll of a graduating class at Vassar, all but two of the women indicated a desire to marry; one said no, the other, maybe. And all but one of the students who wished to marry expressed a desire to have children.

Of course, young people in the middle classes do have emotional problems. But I believe that the tendency to attribute the origins of many of these psychological problems to conflicts and dislocations in the social order has been misleading. It seems to me that American middle-class life is characterized by the same stability as that of the middle class in Vienna before World War I. I believe that those people who apply the term "crisis of ego identity" almost routinely to any neurotic problem of adolescence would do well to pay more attention to Erikson's comment: "In some young people, in some classes, at some periods of history, this crisis will be minimal. . . ."[19]

Implications for Higher Education

In recent years, due to pressures such as the sharp competition for entrance into "select" colleges and recognition of the waste of intellectual resources (because many bright young people fail to go to college or to finish after they enter), educators have become increasingly interested in the personal qualities of students. Accordingly, they now pay considerable attention to what psychiatrists and other representatives of the psychological sciences have to say about personality characteristics.

It is one thing to present to educators the view that the ma-

[19] Erikson, Erik H. *Young Man Luther.* New York: Norton, 1958, p. 14.

jority of students are late adolescents who are experiencing a crisis of ego identity involving instability of mood, sexual problems, confusions of social status and role, and the like. It is quite another to propound the notion that the trouble with many, if not most, college students (perhaps especially college women) is the opposite—that is, a relative absence of problems, anxieties, and difficulties, an identity too readily and too easily assumed. Obviously, the implications of these two opposing points of view for education are vastly different.

Psychoanalysis and dynamic psychology are the heirs of clinical practice. They originated in attempts to reduce suffering, to mitigate symptoms, to introduce unity and wholeness into the personality. And although there is hardly a realm of thought or activity, from artistic creativity to politics, about which representatives of these fields have not had something valuable to say, clinical activity and practice are still their main endeavors. When psychoanalysts, psychiatrists, and psychologists are called upon by educators to tell them something about students, what emerges usually is a doctrine centered on mental health as stability or the reduction of symptoms or anxieties: Free the student from his blocks or anxieties, and he will study better, think better, and in general function better in his role as student. Of course, for students with neurotic problems or difficulties, such an outlook is appropriate.

But what does this tell the educator about the many students who have few anxieties and problems? The implication, I suppose, is that such students, those who display no neurotic symptoms, will somehow develop well. Perhaps the philosophic basis of such an outlook is what might be termed "natural growth"—that is, the view that, if the proper milieu is provided and the blocks to progress removed, the individual has forces within himself that will propel him to go on developing. But does this indeed happen? The research of the Mellon Foundation raises considerable doubt.

Consider two alumnae of Vassar College who were studied by the Mellon Foundation four years after their graduation.

> Shortly after graduation, Miss G. married a poultry farmer in upstate New York. She now has two sons and, as she puts it, has

"settled into a small-town routine." When asked whether she feels any obligation to pursue activities outside of the home as a consequence of her education, she replied as follows: "No, I don't. I think the reason for this is that I am so seldom reminded —actively—that I've had the education. In other words, I don't see the people, you know, who've had education, who expect anything of me. Sometimes, though, it does pass through my mind. I wonder if I am making use of it well enough, and then I think about it. I think my general attitude is that I've been broadened by my education; and right now there is really nothing concrete I can do, because I feel so strongly that my place is in the home."

Her classmate, Miss M., who came of a social-register family, had married one year after graduation and lived with her husband and daughter in an elegant apartment in New York City. She said that she "couldn't be happier" and "things went along without a hitch." When asked what she thought college had contributed to her current life, she replied: "The different interests it opened—some things I wish I had more time for now. It made me much more curious, taught me how to study." And then she added, "I don't know how it affects my life at the moment."

From a mental-hygiene point of view, these young women are a dream. They manifest no tensions, no anxieties, none of the sense of dissatisfaction one sometimes sees in graduates of prominent women's colleges who are confined to the home by small children and who wonder whether they should be putting their education to nobler use. One would hardly begrudge these women their contentment, and it must be granted that they are excellent wives and mothers. But it is difficult, nevertheless, to accept their complacency. Given the present condition of the United States and of the world, it seems that American society has the right to expect more of its most intelligent and best-educated women than that they live happy and secure family lives and contribute to the population explosion. Neither of these young women was interested in politics, and there was nothing to suggest that they were more developed intellectually or ideologically than they had been as college seniors. If the capacity for continued development is considered an important educational goal—and many college catalogues list it as one—then college has in some way failed in the case of these two women.[20]

Cases such as these suggest that the "natural growth" point of view may have some limitations. Conditions of development that impose little strain often produce a personality that is stable and integrated but lacking in depth or complexity. If mental health, viewed as the absence of symptoms, is the primary concern, then one can be satisfied with the two women just described. But if the goals of personality development are more complex and diverse, there is cause for alarm. In Ernest Jones's opinion, for example, the psychologically healthy mind is one in which the full capacities are available for use.

These considerations have led Sanford to suggest that higher education be viewed as a process of challenge and response:

> It seems that if growth is to occur at the college level . . . something has to happen to make it occur. We have to introduce stimuli which challenge the individual to make new responses and thus to expand his personality. This point of view seems to be in accordance with that of most educators, but it tends to be opposed by parents and many psychotherapists, who, far from thinking of ways to upset people, are rather on the lookout for ways to calm them down. Of course, it must be added that the kind of strain that can induce growth or development must be one which does not exceed certain limits. Undoubtedly, strains which are too severe will force the individual to fall back on earlier or more primitive responses and will lead to no gain at all. Whereas I should not like to underestimate the number of young people who are not growing because they have to deal with strains beyond their adaptive capacities, I should not want our preoccupation with maladjustment to blind us to the fundamental principle of growth and development, which is that of challenge and response.[21]

[20] It must be recognized, of course, that these women were quite young when they were studied as alumnae. It is possible that qualities of depth and complexity of intellect and personality that are not now evident may emerge in time.

[21] Sanford, Nevitt. A Psychologist Speculates about New Perspectives.

Katz and Sanford have submitted proposals for a college curriculum that is based on the challenge-and-response theory of learning and personality development in students.[22]

The challenge-and-response theory of education so outlined is based on the notion that "under conditions of comfort and protection the inclination to go on using old responses is very strong. One might say that it is natural to grow, but it is also natural to stand still."[23]

In short, if the goal is maximum differentiation and complexity in the personality as well as stability and integration, the contributions of the psychological sciences to the theory and practice of higher education must be submitted to considerable reevaluation. The theory that personality development is most enhanced by conditions that impose the least stress upon the individual simply cannot be assumed to be valid.[24] Max Hutt and Daniel Miller say, for example, "The ideal training would seem to be one which provides the utmost consistency in ideals, historical prototypes, and objects of identification."[25] The greater Viennese society (as opposed to its stable middle class) prior to World War I had almost none of these things. Instead there were censorship, anti-Semitism, and violent class conflict. And it was essentially Vienna that produced Hitler. But, as Lionel Trilling points out,[26] Vienna also produced

---

In Patterson, Franklin (Ed.). *The Adolescent Citizen.* Glencoe, Illinois: Free Press, 1960, pp. 276–277.

[22] Katz, Joseph, and Sanford, Nevitt. The Curriculum in the Perspective of the Theory of Personality Development. In Sanford, Nevitt (Ed.). *The American College.*

[23] See Sanford. A Psychologist Speculates about New Perspectives.

[24] I should like to make clear that by challenge or stress I do not mean simply hard work. If anything, students are worked too hard at most prominent colleges in the name of standards, excellence, or competition with China, or to avoid the draft. Many students are so burdened by their attempts to meet routine academic demands that they have neither the time nor the energy to respond to the supposed liberating stimulation of liberal education. See Chapter 2.

[25] Hutt, Max L., and Miller, Daniel R. Value Interiorization and Personality Development. *Journal of Social Issues,* 1949, **5**, 27.

[26] Trilling, Lionel. *Freud and the Crisis of Our Culture.* Boston: Beacon Press, 1958.

Freud. I am hardly anxious to see another Hitler, but I should like to see some more Freuds. It is ironic that psychoanalysis and dynamic psychology, which had their origins in the fullest recognition of the sense of possibility and variousness in man, should, in their application to theories and practices of higher education, be interpreted and used in ways that serve to limit experience and circumscribe consciousness.

5

Personality Development after College

I have argued in Chapter 1 that the changes in personality which occur during the college years tend to have considerable persistence. William James[1] remarked: "Outside of their own business, the ideas gained by men before they are twenty-five are practically the only ideas they shall have in their lives." Yet this view of the permanence of personality change of the college years is by no means widely held. Many faculty members believe that even when students are liberalized by college experience, their attitudes and values are likely to "regress" toward conventional beliefs once they leave the shelter of college life. This issue of the permanence of change introduced into students by college experience is, of course, a very profound—perhaps the most profound—educational issue. In the long run, the best evaluation of the effects of higher education will come from studies of alumni, that is, from studies of the long-range consequences of college. This chapter presents some research findings bearing on this question. The research is based on samples of Vassar

[1] James, William. *The Principles of Psychology*. New York: Holt, 1890, Vol. 2, p. 411.

College women in three classes who were tested as seniors and who were retested three or four years after graduation.

Unlike the situation of the undergraduate years, there is a dearth of research dealing with personality change after college or with the relationships between characteristics of undergraduates and alumni. Except for Edward Strong's studies of interests,[2] there are only three publications concerned with studies of attitudes and opinions of the same individuals as students and later as alumni. Erland Nelson administered a conservatism-radicalism questionnaire to 3,758 students at a variety of colleges, and in 1950 he repeated the testing with 901 of his original subjects. He discovered a post-college trend toward "slightly more liberalism" over the 14-year test-retest period; but for the most part, the results indicated that the original positions were maintained with a considerable degree of consistency.[3] B. Richard Bugelski and Olive Lester[4] and Theodore Newcomb[5] carried out similar studies involving shorter time intervals between the original testing and the retest. By and large, their results support Nelson's conclusions about the persistence of tendencies after graduation.

There has been one study that is personality-centered, rather than attitude- or opinion-centered. Mildred Tate and Virginia Musick[6] tested 92 seniors at Virginia Polytechnic Institute in 1940–41 and retested 80 of them in 1947–48. The measures involved were a personal adjustment scale devised by Tate and the Bernreuter Personality Inventory. On the latter, the graduates scored lower on neuroticism and higher on extraversion and dominance. The repe-

[2] Strong, Edward K., Jr. *Changes of Interests with Age.* Stanford, Calif.: Stanford University Press, 1931; *Vocational Interests of Men and Women.* Stanford, Calif.: Stanford University Press, 1943; Permanence of Interest Scores over Twenty-Two Years. *Journal of Applied Psychology,* 1951, **35,** 89–91; *Vocational Interests Eighteen Years after College.* Minneapolis: University of Minnesota Press, 1955.

[3] Nelson. Persistence of Attitudes.

[4] Bugelski and Lester. Changes in Attitude in a Group of College Students.

[5] Newcomb. *Personality and Social Change.*

[6] Tate, Mildred, and Musick, Virginia. Adjustment Problems of College Students. *Social Forces,* 1954, **33,** 182–185.

tition of the personal adjustment scale revealed fewer problems for the subjects as graduates than as students.

As part of the research procedures of the Mellon Foundation at Vassar College, samples of alumnae in three different graduating classes were tested with the same battery that had been administered to them as seniors. One class was tested three years after graduation, the other two when four years had elapsed. The test batteries differed somewhat for the three classes but included two administrations of the California F (Authoritarianism) and E (Ethnocentrism) Scales[7] and the Vassar Attitude Inventory.[8] The Vassar Attitude Inventory contains the following scales: Developmental Status,[9] Impulse Expression,[10] Social Maturity,[11] Dominance and Confidence, Social Integration, Masculine Role, and Repression and Suppression. As indicated in the preceding chapters, seniors score significantly lower than freshmen on the F and E Scales and significantly higher on the Developmental Status, Impulse Expression, and Social Maturity Scales. Seniors and freshmen do not differ significantly on the remaining scales of the Vassar Attitude Inventory.

The Developmental Status Scale is made up of items that distinguish younger from older students. High scorers (seniors) in comparison with low scorers (freshmen) are flexible and uncompulsive, less censorious of people but more critical of the institutional authority of family, state, or religion; high scorers are also more intraceptive, nonconforming, free of cynicism, realistic, and mature in interests.

On the Impulse Expression Scale, high scorers, in contrast to low scorers, display greater readiness to express impulses or to seek gratification of them in overt action or in conscious feeling and

[7] Adorno *et al. The Authoritarian Personality.*

[8] Webster, Harold, Freedman, Mervin, and Sanford, Nevitt. *Research Manual for VC Attitude Inventory and VC Figure Preference Test.* Poughkeepsie, N.Y.: Mary Conover Mellon Foundation, Vassar College, 1957.

[9] Webster. Changes in Attitude during College.

[10] Sanford *et al.* Impulse Expression as a Variable of Personality.

[11] Webster *et al.* A New Instrument for Studying Authoritarianism in Personality.

attitude. High scorers are dominant, aggressive, autonomous, exhibitionistic, and they express interest in sex, excitement, and change.

The Social Maturity Scale provides a measure of authoritarianism that is less ideological than the original F Scale. Low scorers are authoritarian, compulsive, rigid, punitive, submissive to power, conventional, cynical, anti-intellectual, and emotionally constricted.

The Vassar samples involved are alumnae of the classes of 1954, 1955, and 1956, numbering 78, 74, and 79 respondents respectively. The class of 1956 was tested three years after graduation, the other two classes after four years had elapsed. The majority of subjects were obtained by writing to women selected at random from the list of the graduating class. However, each alumnae sample contains returns for some 15 to 20 women who were tested at alumnae reunions rather than by the mail procedure. Of course, not all of the alumnae included in the original samples returned their tests; completions amounted to some 60 to 70 per cent of the total number sent out.

Since all of the alumnae had been tested as seniors, we can evaluate the extent to which the samples of alumnae are representative of their senior classes.[12] Knowledge of the representativeness of the alumnae respondents at the time they were seniors, however, does not exclude the possibility that they have undergone significantly different experiences since graduation. One important factor here is marriage. If married students were appreciably over or underrepresented in the samples under consideration, potential bias might be introduced. Nowadays, about three-quarters of a class is married within the four years subsequent to graduation, and the

[12] The mean on the F Scale of the total senior class of 1956 is slightly smaller at the .05 level of significance than the mean of the responding group, but this is not the case for the class of 1955, where there is no significant difference. (A statistical difference significant "at the .05 level" is a difference that could occur accidentally or randomly [that is, not arise from a systematic cause] only 5 per cent of the time, were it possible to repeat the experiment in the same way a large number of times. Similarly, a difference "significant at the .01 level" will be an accidental finding only once in a hundred such experiments. The same holds true for other levels of significance that are chosen a priori by the statistician for the purpose of discovering true differences, as opposed to those that are likely to result only from random fluctuation.)

breakdown of married versus unmarried alumnae in the classes of 1954 and 1955 approaches this figure fairly closely. The class of 1956, however, appears to contain a somewhat larger proportion of unmarried students (47 per cent) than would be expected three years after graduation.

For the three classes that were tested as both seniors and alumnae, only the Repression and Suppression Scale displays a significant mean change, the alumnae in two classes scoring higher. The Social Integration Scale, which is highly correlated with Repression and Suppression, shows the same trend but less markedly. An upward trend in scores on the Social Maturity Scale is also evident, though it is statistically significant (.05 level) for only one class.

On the Repression and Suppression Scale, a high score indicates a tendency to reject items which seem strange or unconventional. A low scorer endorses items which convey an impression of imprudence, unconventionality, and lack of inhibition.

High scorers on the Social Integration Scale are likely to be conventional and to be free of feelings of social alienation; low scorers describe themselves as unhappy social isolates.

Are these mean trends characteristic of most students in the sample, or are they accounted for by extreme shifts on the part of a few? Table 1, which gives the proportions of the total sample of alumnae changing in either direction, shows that the significant mean trends are indeed typical of the majority of the alumnae sampled. In addition, a significantly large proportion of students are found to decline in scores on the Impulse Expression Scale, the changes evidently being of insufficient magnitude to produce a significant mean change.

Senior-alumnae returns on the Minnesota Multiphasic Personality Inventory[13] are available for one class, the class of 1955, retested in 1959. There is an over-all trend toward lower scores for the alumnae on the clinical scales, five of the changes being statistically significant: at the .01 level for the Hypochondriasis, Psychasthenia, Schizophrenia, and Mania Scales, and at the .05 level for the Hysteria Scale.

[13] Hathaway and McKinley. *Manual for the Minnesota Multiphasic Personality Inventory.*

TABLE 1

PROPORTIONS OF ALUMNAE CHANGING IN INDICATED DIRECTIONS FROM SENIOR TO ALUMNAE TESTS: POOLED RESULTS FOR CLASSES OF 1954 AND 1955 ($N = 193$)

	Scales						
Direction of Change	Social Maturity	Impulse Expression	Developmental Status	Repression and Suppression	Social Integration	Dominance and Confidence	Masculine Role
Increase	60*	39	42	64*	62*	50	44
No Change	03	01	05	03	04	05	05
Decrease	37	60*	53	33	34	45	51

* Significant at the .05 level.

Similar "positive" trends characterize results obtained with the California Psychological Inventory,[14] which was administered to seniors in 1956 and to alumnae in 1959. The alumnae score significantly higher, at the .01 level, on the following scales: Achievement via Independence, Sense of Well-Being, Self-Control, and Psychological-Mindedness. They also outscore seniors at the .05 level on the Responsibility Scale.

When married and unmarried alumnae are compared with respect to differences in change, the only significant result involves the Impulse Expression Scale. For the class of 1955, the married alumnae decline on Impulse Expression and the unmarried alumnae increase so that the difference between changes is significant at the .001 level. The same trend appeared for the class of 1954, but it was not significant.

Probably the most significant finding in considering the senior-alumnae comparisons is that there is no indication of a consistent tendency over a period of three or four years after graduation for the alumnae to change appreciably on the major attitude dimensions tapped by the Vassar Attitude Inventory. The shifts toward

[14] Gough. *Manual for the California Psychological Inventory.*

decreased authoritarianism and increased impulse expression and rebelliousness, so marked during the undergraduate years, are neither continued nor reversed during the early postcollege years.

One trend that does appear to reverse itself, however, is the trend that had been observed during the college years toward increased emotionality and psychopathology, as shown for instance by a slight general increase in Minnesota Multiphasic Personality Inventory scores. During the postcollege years, the trend shown by these and California Psychological Inventory scores is toward "normalcy" or conventional good adjustment. The changes on the Repression and Suppression and the Social Integration Scales of the Vassar Attitude Inventory are perhaps best interpreted in this light also. Although they were originally developed as validity scales, independent unpublished factor analyses by Harold Webster and by Carl Bereiter have agreed in showing that they are substantive scales. The factor accounting for most of their variance was identified as "inhibition" (of symptoms or complaints) by Webster and as a "sense of social and emotional well-being" by Bereiter. These results are based on students in college, however, and it may be that a more simple kind of social desirability accounts for a major part of the variance in tests of this kind when they are administered by mail, outside the college setting. The evidence for a benign trend in mental health among alumnae, plausible as it seems, must therefore be accepted with some reservation.

The differential change on the Impulse Expression Scale of the married and the unmarried alumnae is interesting, for it accords very well with images of the freer, less stable existence of the young unmarried woman in contrast to the more secure but more restrained existence of the young wife. The results suggest that, in studies of the postcollege years, biographical variables related to way of life may be of considerable importance.

Evidence that changes in outlook and opinion occur after graduation was presented in Chapter 1. Herbert Hyman and Paul Sheatsley[15] have pointed out that during the McCarthy period, that

[15] Hyman, Herbert H., and Sheatsley, Paul B. Trends in Public Opinion on Civil Liberties. *Journal of Social Issues,* 1953, **9**, 6–16.

is, around 1953, restrictive sentiment concerning the exercise of traditional American freedoms increased among college alumni. Contemporary events can effect changes in beliefs and attitudes among college alumni. The studies of Vassar alumnae reported in this chapter, however, suggest that such changes are neither frequent nor large. Empirical research indicates that the changes in personality which occur in the college years persist for at least three or four years after graduation.

6

Attitude Contrasts of Educated Women over Six Decades

Changes in the climate of American opinion and in the character structure of Americans are perennial topics of interest and curiosity for observers of our social scene. In the last century, such observers were likely to be men of letters: Alexis de Tocqueville, Mark Twain, and Henry James come to mind as a few examples. In recent years, since World War I and particularly in the last generation, this function has been assumed increasingly by social scientists. They and the critics rather than the creative writers have been the ones to tell us what is going on in American life. It is difficult to think of a novel that tells us as much about what it is like to be a woman today as *The Bostonians*[1] told about what it was like to be a feminist in 1875. Nowadays one is likely to read Simone de Beauvoir or Margaret Mead instead.

For the most part, earlier analysts of long-term trends in American culture had to operate without the benefit of what we now regard as indispensable material in a proper study of people or social events—that is, interviews, questionnaires, planned observa-

[1] James, Henry. *The Bostonians.* New York: Dial, 1945.

tion, and the like. Such techniques were little utilized prior to the thirties, and only since the end of World War II has any sizable and complex body of data been built up systematically for use in the newer social sciences, such as cultural anthropology, psychology, and sociology. The activities of the Mellon Foundation at Vassar College[2] provided an opportunity for just such systematic research into some of the general changes in American culture over the past half-century. As part of the research program, opinions and attitudes of Vassar alumnae of various periods going back as far as the class of 1904 were explored.[3]

One of the instruments used by the Mellon Foundation to measure the kinds of changes that take place in undergraduate students was the California Public Opinion Survey[4]—the 60-item questionnaire containing the familiar F and E Scales, consisting of 32 and 20 items respectively, and the eight-item PEC Scale.[5] The F Scale was, of course, developed as a measure of authoritarianism, a personality syndrome which is predictive of behavior in a variety of situations. Among many traits which have been subsumed under the rubric of authoritarianism are compulsiveness, rigidity, intolerance of ambiguity, punitive morality, submission to power, conventionality, cynicism, and anti-intraception. The E Scale is a measure of the related phenomenon of ethnocentrism—the disposition to glorify in-groups, family, country, social class, and the like, while attributing negative qualities to out-groups, for example, Negroes or foreigners. The PEC (Political Economic Conservatism) Scale has been found to possess little reliability as a scale, chiefly because of its brevity, and in our studies no attempt has been made to deal with PEC scores as such. The items of the scale have been utilized for their individual contributions, however.

[2] Sanford (Ed.). Personality Development during the College Years, *The American College.*

[3] Freedman, Mervin. A Half-Century of Vassar Opinion. *Vassar Alumnae Magazine,* 1959, **44,** 3–6; Studies of College Alumni.

[4] Adorno *et al. The Authoritarian Personality.*

[5] The questionnaire was administered with the standard instructions. For each item respondents may select any position from plus three to minus three to indicate degree of agreement or disagreement with the sentiment expressed. Zero or neutral responses are discouraged.

In order to obtain data on alumnae comparable with those available for current students, the California Public Opinion Survey was included among the tests and questionnaires administered to the alumnae groups that were studied. This chapter is concerned specifically with comparisons among the various alumnae groups and between the alumnae groups and current students on the F and E Scales. Some comparisons using individual items will also be reported.

The classes and numbers involved are:

1. Eighty-five members of the class of 1904, almost the entire class of alumnae surviving in 1958.

2. Forty-three members of the class of 1914, tested at a class reunion. How representative these women are of their entire class is, of course, debatable. As we shall see shortly, however, alumnae who attend reunions appear to yield test results much like those obtained from alumnae who do not attend reunions but who respond to invitations by mail to cooperate in a scientific survey.

3. Seventy-three alumnae of the classes of 1921–24. Sixteen were tested at a reunion. The remaining 57 are members of the class of 1923 who responded to mail invitations to participate.[6]

4. Fifty members of the classes of 1929–35 who participated in a three-day assessment study at Vassar College.

5. Seventy-seven alumnae of the classes of 1940–43. Thirty were tested at a class reunion, the remaining 47 being members of the class of 1943 who responded by mail.[7]

6. Finally, 200 members of the class of 1956, chosen at random from a total sample of 378, the latter figure comprising almost the total graduating class.

The returns of the classes of 1929–35 were obtained in 1954. The class of 1956 was tested shortly before graduation. The remaining returns were obtained between 1957 and 1959.

Before reporting our results, some attention to the general na-

[6] The two separate means differ by only .01 of a point, the standard deviations differing by 3.09, an insignificant amount.

[7] The additional 47 returns yielded a mean 4.67 points greater and a standard deviation 4.29 points lower, neither difference approaching significance.

ture of the samples is in order. First, of course, we are dealing only with women, and with the kind who go to colleges like Vassar—very intelligent women of relatively favored socioeconomic backgrounds. Not much is known about variations in the backgrounds or characteristics of women who have gone to college in various decades of this century. However, we do know that now, as compared with the early years of the century, Vassar has fewer students whose parents are clergymen, teachers, or in literary professions. The percentage of professional versus business backgrounds has not changed, but the nature of the professions has. Now law and medicine are more heavily represented. Since 1930 more foreign students and members of minority groups, particularly Jews, have been accepted as students, although the proportion of such students is still fairly low. Considering everything, the samples seem to possess a degree of homogeneity of background that would seldom be found in studies designed to cover so wide an age range.

It should be noted that our samples of alumnae are confined to women who are members, although not necessarily active ones, of the alumnae association. Those graduates who have maintained no contact with Vassar College in recent years are not represented. Sixty to 70 per cent of the alumnae to whom letters were sent responded by completing and returning the tests, and, of course, the extent to which the results of the nonrespondents may differ from those reported here is unknown.

Table 2 presents the means and standard deviations on the F Scale for each of the above-mentioned groups. Several trends are

TABLE 2

MEANS AND STANDARD DEVIATIONS ON THE F SCALE

Class(es)	*N*	$\overline{x}$	SD
1904	85	121.14	35.84
1914	43	99.53	33.99
1921–24	73	100.96	28.86
1929–35	50	87.98	22.15
1940–43	77	87.56	24.44
1956	200	95.09	23.87

immediately apparent. The class of 1904 scores easily significantly higher (according to the *t* test) than any other group. The class of 1914 and those of the early twenties are paired with the next highest means, which are less than a point apart. The thirties and the forties classes are the groups with the lowest means. The mean of the class of 1956 differs from those of the thirties and forties classes at the .05 level of significance.[8] The class of 1956 ranks significantly lower than that of 1904, but not significantly lower than that of 1914 or those of the early twenties. In short, we find 1904 to be highest on the F Scale, 1914 and the twenties paired as the next highest, and the early thirties and forties lowest of all, preceding a significant rise for the class of 1956.

I do not consider these results to be merely the product of a tendency to agree with fatuous and bombastic statements—that is, a matter of response set. Recent work by Donald Brown and Lois-Ellen Datta,[9] Harold Webster,[10] and Richard Christie, Joan Havel, and Bernard Seidenberg[11] demonstrates that authoritarianism cannot be explained by response set alone. Thus, for a sample of Vassar students, a highly reliable and experimentally independent measure of response set (KR 21 = .93) has a correlation of only .26 with the F Scale.[12]

An interesting finding is the discovery that the earlier groups are likely to adopt more extreme positions in response to individual items. This finding lends support to the notion that, as compared with earlier periods in our history, the recent American scene has been characterized by less fixity and greater flexibility of opinion—or, perhaps, by greater conformity and homogeneity of opinion.

[8] See Footnote 12, Chapter 5, for an explanation of the meaning of levels of significance of statistical differences.

[9] Brown, Donald R., and Datta, Lois-Ellen. Authoritarianism, Verbal Ability, and Response Set. *Journal of Abnormal and Social Psychology,* 1959, **58,** 131–134.

[10] Webster, Harold. Correcting Personality Scales for Response Sets or Suppression Effects. *Psychological Bulletin,* 1958, **55,** 62–64.

[11] Christie, Richard, Havel, Joan, and Seidenberg, Bernard. Is the F Scale Irreversible? *Journal of Abnormal and Social Psychology,* 1958, **56,** 143–158.

[12] Webster *et al. Research Manual for VC Attitude Inventory and VC Figure Preference Test.*

As one would anticipate, and as Table 3 indicates, results for the E Scale display a similar pattern. The class of 1904 ranks highest of all, significantly higher than those of 1914 and 1921–24 at the .01 level. The means of 1929–35 and 1940–43 differ from the

TABLE 3

MEANS AND STANDARD DEVIATIONS ON THE E SCALE

Class(es)	*N*	$\overline{x}$	SD
1904	85	64.30	27.58
1914	43	47.86	23.41
1921–24	73	48.92	21.37
1929–35	50	44.36	17.03
1940–43	77	41.70	16.45
1956	200	44.70	17.97

mean of the early twenties at the .17 and .02 levels of significance respectively. Unlike the situation with the F Scale, however, there is no significant rise on the Ethnocentrism Scale for the class of 1956.

How do we account for the fact that alumnae of some classes and decades differ widely from those of others in the kind of general outlook measured by these scales? Is it due to chronological age —that is, is it a matter of experience that is a function of a certain time of life? Is it a result of childhood conditioning, a predisposition to a particular outlook in adulthood as a consequence of having been a child at a certain period of American life? To what extent is current outlook a reflection of the influence of schooling, chiefly perhaps, college experience? It is difficult, of course, to attempt answers to such questions.

We do, however, possess some leads. First, I am inclined to rule out chronological age as a cogent explanatory factor. While one could account for differences between groups of women widely separated in age on such a basis, this hardly explains the large differences that are found between members of adjacent decades, for example, between the classes of 1904 and 1914, or 1921–24 and 1929–35. Why should women averaging seventy-four years of age at the time of testing respond differently from women who are sixty-six, or why should women of forty-seven at the time of testing differ from those who are forty-three?

The matter of the contribution of childhood experience to test scores in later life is, of course, one on which little empirical information can be brought directly to bear. My general view of the matter would be that, at least in recent times, American culture has not been strongly authoritarian. If that is so, then only a minority of individuals have undergone the kinds of childhood experiences delineated in *The Authoritarian Personality,*[13] experiences which would be expected to lead to rigid fixation upon authoritarian sentiments. To put this in another way, I am inclined to think that most individuals who express somewhat authoritarian views are still open to new experience and the possibility of change; and in educated people, I believe that the period of greatest change in general social outlook is likely to be the college years. Events at large on the national or international scene often have considerable influence upon the attitudes of college students, as we shall see shortly, when we consider the individual items of the California Public Opinion Survey.

In short, I consider experiences of the college years to be a major source of the decade-by-decade variations in attitudes which we have observed. Increasing liberalization of social outlook in American culture during the years of this century has in general been reflected in comparable changes in college students. And these changes have apparently persisted after college.

Results obtained with current students support this theory. Incoming freshman classes at Vassar yield means on F ranging from 115 to 118, with a standard deviation of about 25. Means for graduating seniors cluster around 95, with a standard deviation of about 24. Some evidence that the sentiments expressed by seniors persist with little or no change is provided in Table 4. It may be seen that, when alumnae who were given the F and E Scales as seniors are retested three and four years later, there is very little change.[14]

[13] Adorno *et al.*
[14] See Chapter 5.

TABLE 4

Means and Standard Deviations on the F and E Scales for Alumnae Who Were Tested as Seniors

Scale	Class	*N*	Date of Retest	Seniors	Alumnae
F	1955	74	1959	$\bar{x}$ 91.16 SD 23.36	$\bar{x}$ 93.62 SD 24.60
F	1956	79	1959	$\bar{x}$ 99.34 SD 21.94	$\bar{x}$ 96.14 SD 22.00
E	1955	74	1959	$\bar{x}$ 44.69 SD 15.49	$\bar{x}$ 45.37 SD 17.23
E	1956	79	1959	$\bar{x}$ 45.56 SD 17.76	$\bar{x}$ 44.84 SD 14.87

But perhaps study of the individual items provides the most support for the notion that the tenor of the times at which the alumnae were in college is intimately related to the attitudes they now display.[15] Consider the item "What this country needs most, more than laws and political programs, is a few courageous, tireless, devoted leaders in whom the people can put their faith." As Table 5 indicates, the forties classes are the only group in which the majority, 57 per cent, reject this view of leadership. In a similar vein, the early forties classes are the group most emphatic in rejecting the notion "Obedience and respect for authority are the most important virtues that children should learn," with 77 per cent responding negatively. In comparison with the forties, the differences are significant for 1904, 1914, and 1956 ($p < .19$ for the classes of 1921–24).

The classes of 1940–43 respond most negatively to the statement "Now that a new world organization is set up, America must be sure that she loses none of her independence and complete power

[15] The significance of the difference between groups for scores on individual items has been calculated by the chi square technique, utilizing two-by-four tables rather than two-by-six tables. The "two" and "three" response categories at each extreme have been combined, because in the smaller samples of alumnae expected frequencies in the "three" cells fall below the acceptable levels for calculation of chi square.

TABLE 5

PERCENTAGES OF REJECTION OF SELECTED ITEMS OF THE CALIFORNIA PUBLIC OPINION SURVEY

Item	1904 $N=85$	1914 $N=43$	1921–24 $N=73$	1929–35 $N=50$	1940–43 $N=77$	1956 $N=200$
What this country needs most, more than laws and political programs, is a few courageous, tireless, devoted leaders in whom the people can put their faith.	17	49	32	42	57	44
Obedience and respect for authority are the most important virtues that children should learn.	35	49	62	70	77	51
Now that a new world organization is set up, America must be sure that she loses none of her independence and complete power as a sovereign nation.	34	72	66	75	82	58
Human nature being what it is, there will always be war and conflict.	44	47	21	32	37	30
It is only natural and right for each person to think that his family is better than any other.	62	65	78	66	69	52
Someday it will probably be shown that astrology can explain a lot of things.	81	87	78	94	94	80
Science has its place, but there are many important things that can never possibly be understood by the human mind.	29	58	37	53	42	39

as a sovereign nation," with 82 per cent of the group expressing disagreement. Here the early forties differ significantly from 1904 and 1956, with the difference from 1921–24 approaching significance (.08 level). In the case of the item "Human nature being what it is, there will always be war and conflict," the early forties are closest to 1914 and 1904 in expressing disapproval. Forty-seven per cent of the class of 1914 reject the item, 44 per cent of 1904, and 37 per cent of 1940–43, with the remaining groups expressing disapproval by smaller margins.

The above comparisons and the fact that the classes of 1940–43 have the lowest E Scale scores of any group would seem to reflect American attitudes in the years just prior to and during World War II: optimistic views of man's potential and of postwar society, fervent internationalism, and alertness to the possibility and dangers of dictatorship or authoritarian rule.

As a sidelight, it is interesting to note that the generally liberal position of the alumnae of the early forties in social and broadly political matters is not accompanied by anything approaching economic liberalism or radicalism. Vassar alumnae in general adhere to conservative economic values, but even in this company, the alumnae of the early forties are distinguished by their conservatism. Fully 92 per cent of the group reject the statement "It is up to the government to make sure that everyone has a secure job and a good standard of living." The majority of alumnae of the early thirties oppose this idea also, but as one would expect, by a smaller majority, that is, 72 per cent.

Similarly, the views of current students may to a considerable extent be regarded as reflections or functions of certain large-scale trends in American life. Turning again to the item "Obedience and respect for authority are the most important virtues that children should learn," we find that only 51 per cent of the class of 1956 reject this item, in comparison with 77 per cent for the classes of 1940–43 and 70 per cent for the classes of 1929–35 ($p < .001$ and $< .17$, respectively). One has to go back to 1914 and 1904 to find smaller percentages of rejection than that of 1956, 49 per cent and 35 per cent respectively. "It is only natural and right for each person to think that his family is better than any other"; Table 5 indicates that the class of 1956 rejects this statement by the smallest majority of any group.[16]

"Someday it will probably be shown that astrology can explain a lot of things." Eighty per cent of the class of 1956 disagree as compared with 78 per cent for the early twenties. The margin of disagreement is greater for all other groups ($p < .08$ for the difference between 1956 and 1914).

In general, we may see in the above comparisons of the class of 1956 with the other groups some of the smugness and the attachment to the status quo which was characteristic of many segments of American society a decade ago. Similarly we may discern some of the irrationality, the phony romanticism, perhaps, that was prominent at the time, as evident in certain shallow religious revivals.

If we consider the California Public Opinion Survey, particularly the F Scale, in its more purely psychological aspects—that is, if we think of it as telling us something about the nature of the personality (as a clue to the way in which inner impulses are handled, and as an index of the amount of self-insight possessed by the subject)—the conclusion seems obvious that social and individual psychological processes parallel one another rather closely. Changes in American society and culture seem to be accompanied by changes in individual personality structure, as well as by changes of opinion and attitude.

[16] The difference between 1956 and the classes of 1929–35 is significant, and the difference between 1956 and 1940–43 approaches significance ($p < .07$).

III
SEXUALITY

7

Sex among College Students: A Contemporary Report

In all things, and perhaps particularly in matters of sex, it is important to be aware of the common humanity of men and women. Nevertheless, empirical studies of sexual behavior and attitudes among college men and women indicate that there are substantial differences between them. They often differ considerably in matters such as rates of sexual intercourse and the need for emotional intimacy in a sexual relationship.

The sexual behavior of college women has undergone more variation than that of men in the last two generations; and its study tells a great deal about changes in American character and society since 1900. Unfortunately, accurate information about the sexual attitudes and behavior of college women has been hard to come by. Examination of the scientific literature reveals few studies of either sex—and in these studies, the subjects are usually men. Presumably men are considered better subjects. They probably have less inhibition about participating in a study of sexual behavior or attitudes; and it is less likely that parents or agents who act in loco parentis, for example, college authorities, will rise up in righteous indignation if the sex lives of their male rather than their female charges are subjected to scientific scrutiny. Presumably, too, researchers themselves have less inhibition about studying these matters in men than in women.

Sex at an Eastern Women's College

What follows is a report of the results of a study of sexual behavior among a sample of college women, recent graduates of Vassar College. The data were obtained by means of tests and interviews. The subjects who were interviewed comprise a random sample of the student body, and the test data are based on whole classes of students. In contrast, the most prominent previous studies of the sexual behavior of college women—those conducted by Alfred Kinsey and Paul Gebhard and by Winston Ehrmann—have relied on volunteers[1] or on students who were taking a course in "Marriage and the Family."[2]

The major findings of the Vassar study are based on conversations with 49 seniors who were interviewed several times a year beginning in their freshman year. A detailed account of sexual behavior and attitudes was obtained from each of these students as part of an interview called the "developmental history," a psychoanalytically centered biographical history interview. Included in this interview were questions about sexual experience in infancy and childhood, the physiological changes of puberty, dating, and recent and current sexual experiences. In a second senior interview, the "values" interview, sex was discussed at a somewhat more abstract level, from the point of view of ethical, moral, and religious concerns. And in a third senior interview, the "socialization" interview, which concentrated on the less academic aspects of the college experience—for example, college friendships—some questions were asked about observations of the sexual activities of other students.

Can it be assumed that the students responded truthfully when

[1] Kinsey, Alfred C., and Gebhard, Paul H. *Sexual Behavior in the Human Female.* Philadelphia: Saunders, 1953.

[2] Ehrmann, Winston. *Premarital Dating Behavior.* New York: Holt, 1959.

queried about their sexual experiences? The interviewers entertained no doubt on this score. The students had been interviewed several times a year beginning with their freshman year, and by senior year good rapport between most of the subjects and the research staff had been established. No student, for example, refused to reply to any of the questions dealing with sex.[3]

The possibility must still be considered that interviews influence the behavior of the students in ways that make it dubious to generalize results to students who are not interviewed. The interview procedure was designed to minimize the possibility. For example, the bulk of the interviewing was reserved for the senior year, at which time the interviews were less likely to affect appreciably the college experience; and students were interviewed by several staff members so as to minimize interviewer bias and transference effects. Evidence that the interviews did not exert a marked influence on the students is afforded by the test results; as seniors, the students who were interviewed did not differ significantly on any scale from the total class of which they were a part.

The test data are based on three classes of students (one of them the class from which the interview sample was drawn) which were tested shortly after college entrance and retested in the spring of the senior year. Freshman classes contained around 400 students. Only two or three freshmen did not take the tests each year. The senior classes averaged 270–300 students. Of these, 12–15 were not tested each year.

About one-third of the subjects tested came from upper-class families, families in which there had been high social status and a fair amount of wealth for several generations. There was almost no lower-class representation, that is, daughters of laborers or workmen. Lower-middle-class families, in which the father was a clerk, for example, were rare as well—under 5 per cent. Most of the students were upper middle class, the daughters of business and professional men.

[3] Only two students among those who agreed to be interviewed balked at any point in the entire interviewing program. The same question was involved in both cases—the family income.

About 70 per cent of the subjects were Protestant, chiefly Episcopalians and Presbyterians; 20 per cent were Jewish; and 10 per cent were Catholics. When queried about their religious affiliation, only a handful of students reported none or stated that they were atheists or agnostics. About 50 per cent came from the Middle Atlantic states, 20 per cent from the Midwest, and 15 per cent from New England. Of the remainder, the majority came from other regions of the United States; a small number were foreign students. Scores on scholastic aptitude and achievement tests and performance in secondary school indicated that the subjects were highly intelligent, and the great majority valued intellectual accomplishment. The educational backgrounds of the subjects were divided fairly evenly between private and public schools.

Table 6 presents the proportions of the interview sample participating in five categories of sexual behavior: (a) Limited Experience; (b) Restricted Petting; (c) Extensive Petting; (d) Intercourse Confined to Serious Relationships; (e) Uninhibited Behavior. "Limited Experience" consists in behavior that does not go beyond kissing. "Restricted Petting" entails petting "above the waist," to employ a phrase used frequently by students. "Extensive Petting" connotes genital involvement, but not intercourse. "Intercourse Confined to Serious Relationships" means that the subjects had engaged in intercourse in a relationship or relationships involving emotional intimacy. None of the students included in this category had had intercourse with more than two men; in the majority of cases only one man was involved. "Uninhibited Behavior" indicates that sexual intercourse is not confined to men with whom the subject is on terms of emotional intimacy.

Table 6 indicates that the modal category of sexual behavior is Extensive Petting—with a line drawn at intercourse. Restricted Petting contains the second largest number of entries. When combined, these two comprise 68 per cent of the subjects. Twenty-two per cent of the subjects had experienced intercourse, the majority of these in a context of emotional intimacy with the man involved.

Few students had engaged in behavior other than kissing and light petting before the junior and senior years of high school. The modal age for commencing extensive petting was seventeen. Four of

TABLE 6

Sexual Experience of the Interview Sample as of the Senior Year ($N = 49$)

	Limited Experience	Restricted Petting	Extensive Petting	Intercourse Confined to Serious Relationships	Uninhibited Behavior
N	5	13	20	8[a]	3
%	10	27	41	16	6

note: Several of the subjects in the interview sample were married at the time they were interviewed about sexual behavior. The married students have been categorized in accord with their behavior prior to marriage.

[a] Included in this figure are two subjects, each of whom had engaged in intercourse with one man with whom they were not intimately involved emotionally. They had not had intercourse with other men, however.

the 11 nonvirgins had had intercourse prior to college entrance. In keeping with the finding that adults who are particularly active sexually usually start early in life,[4] three of these four students comprise the Uninhibited Behavior group.

In the case of young women who are likely to display affection readily, it is, of course, difficult to define homosexual behavior. If we restrict the sense of the term to sexual behavior with genital involvement, none of the members of the interview sample had been involved in homosexual activities.[5] Two students, however, reported that they enjoyed physical experiences of the hair-combing, back-rubbing kind with other women. One of these women was of the opinion that she would very likely not resist were another woman she thought attractive to make sexual advances to her. Both of these students were among those who were engaging in intercourse with men.

[4] Kinsey and Gebhard. *Sexual Behavior in the Human Female;* Kinsey, Alfred C., Pomeroy, Wardell B., and Martin, Clyde E. *Sexual Behavior in the Human Male.* Philadelphia: Saunders, 1958.

[5] Overt homosexual relations among the student body were observed over the years to be confined chiefly to a very small group, the members of which tended to maintain some distance from the rest of the campus community.

TABLE 7

RESPONSES OF VASSAR FRESHMEN AND SENIORS TO TEST ITEMS CONCERNED WITH SEXUAL BEHAVIOR

Item	Freshmen		Seniors	
	%T	%F	%T	%F
I am embarrassed by dirty stories	20	80***	8	92***
Most people worry too much about sex	43	53	43	57
When a man is with a woman he is usually thinking about things related to her sex	18	78***	29	69**
I have been in trouble one or more times because of my sex behavior	2	98***	6	94***
I wish I were not bothered by thoughts about sex	20	80***	8	90***
A large number of people are guilty of bad sexual conduct	45	51	31	61*
No man of character would ask his fiancée to have sexual intercourse with him before marriage	53	47	18	82***
In illegitimate pregnancies, abortion is in many cases the most reasonable alternative	16	82***	51	49
People would be happier if sex experience before marriage were taken for granted in both men and women	16	84***	35	65*
I like to tell risqué stories	12	84***	25	75***
I like to hear risqué stories	37	63	49	51
I never attend a sexy show if I can avoid it	39	55	12	86***
My sex life is satisfactory	86	10***	80	20***
I have never been in trouble because of my sex behavior	98	2***	86	14***
I am strongly attracted by members of my own sex	8	90***	10	90***
I believe women ought to have as much sexual freedom as men	25	73***	57	41
I have never indulged in any unusual sex practices	90	10***	82	18***
I am worried about sex matters	8	92***	4	96***
Children should be taught all the main facts of sex	90	10***	88	10***
I like to flirt	57	43	84	16***
I like to talk about sex	59	41	69	29**

Item	Freshmen		Seniors	
	%T	%F	%T	%F
Once in a while I laugh at a dirty joke	94	6***	98	2***
Many of my dreams are about sex matters	6	94***	8	92***

NOTE: The percentages presented are pooled means of three classes. (*N*'s for freshman classes are 398, 404, and 392. *N*'s for senior classes are 274, 258, and 253.) All differences between proportions that are significant at the .001 level are significant for all three classes. The other significant differences are significant at the levels indicated for two of the three classes. Where percentages do not total 100, the difference is accounted for by abstentions.

* $p < .05$ ** $p < .01$ *** $p < .001$

In the "developmental history" interview carried out in the senior year, inquiry was made about crushes. The term "crush" was generally interpreted by students to mean intense liking of or admiration for an older girl or young woman, this feeling being tinged with erotic overtones. Fourteen students, 29 per cent of the interview sample, reported experiences of crushes. The objects of these crushes were usually young adults, camp counselors and teachers predominating; occasionally, they were older students. The modal age for crushes was early adolescence, ages twelve to fourteen. Although a number of students enjoyed close relationships with women faculty members, none reported experiencing crushes during the college period. Feelings of admiration for faculty members or older college students apparently lacked the erotic element of the crush.

Most of the subjects were content with their sexual status quo. Table 7 presents the responses of three classes of students to the items pertaining to sex[6] in the battery of tests that they took as freshmen and again as seniors. Table 7 indicates that in response

[6] These items come from: Hathaway and McKinley. *Manual for the Minnesota Multiphasic Personality Inventory;* Gough. *Manual for the California Psychological Inventory;* and Maslow. Self-Esteem (Dominance Feeling) and Sexuality in Women.

to the item "My sex life is satisfactory," the great majority of freshmen and seniors answered "true." In the interview sample, 43 freshmen responded "true," and two "false," with two omissions. Thirty-nine of the seniors said "true," ten replied "false." Of the ten senior responses of "false," three were contributed by students in the Limited Experience category, and three by students in the Restricted Petting category. The four remaining negative responses are divided equally between the Extensive Petting and Intercourse Confined to Serious Relationships categories. This breakdown suggests that there may be some tendency for those students who have had less sexual experience, particularly those in the Limited Experience category, to be dissatisfied.

The interviews bear out the general absence of a sense of frustration, but among the students in the Limited Experience and Restricted Petting categories, there were a number who expressed a desire for more sexual experience. They were unanimous in asserting, however, that they could not or would not seek out physical sexual encounters as such. Sexual gratification, as they saw it, could emerge only in the context of a relationship of some seriousness with a man.

Among the students who had engaged in intercourse the predominant attitude was one of enjoyment and satisfaction. This was particularly true of those young women whose sexual partners were men with whom they shared a close emotional relationship. In fact, among the 11 students who had experienced intercourse, the four who expressed some dissatisfaction with sexual matters were those who were not involved with the men in a serious way. Two of these women were among the three in the Uninhibited Behavior category. One said that she feared her lack of control "might get her into trouble sometime." The other expressed some concern that men valued her "only for my body." The other two students, members of the Intercourse Confined to Serious Relationships category, were regretful because the relationships with the men involved had developed badly. They resented having given themselves to men they no longer cared for or loved. None of the students who had engaged in intercourse reported that they had not enjoyed the physical or sensuous qualities of the experience. None of these young women, moreover, expressed feelings of sinfulness or guilt. None seemed to feel that they had transgressed basic moral or religious codes.

Guilt feelings were, in fact, very little in evidence in the interview sample. There were only two students who expressed strong sentiments of this kind. Both had been "seduced" on one occasion into petting activities that had gone beyond what they considered appropriate. The sense of guilt—shame, the term used by one of the students in referring to her feelings, is perhaps more appropriate—was occasioned in both instances not by the experience as such but rather by its having occurred with men the women did not love. Each of these young women expressed the view that she would not be averse to extensive physical intimacy if she and the man involved cared deeply for one another.

The majority of students who constitute the Extensive Petting category reported feelings of satisfaction with and enjoyment of their sexual activities. Half were engaged or were very seriously involved with the men with whom they were intimate, and in most of these cases only rather vaguely formulated and tenuous prohibitions stood between petting and intercourse. "We've been tempted, naturally," said one, "but we're going to be married, and this is something that can wait." Most of the remaining students in this category, although not engaged or seriously involved, tended to limit their sexual activities to men whom they knew well. There were few who were disposed to distribute their favors on short acquaintance.

Table 7 also indicates that a substantial amount of change in attitudes toward sexual behavior takes place between freshman and senior year. Responses to the following items changed significantly during this period: (a) "A large number of people are guilty of bad sexual conduct." (b) "No man of character would ask his fiancée to have sexual intercourse with him before marriage." (c) "In illegitimate pregnancies abortion is in many cases the most reasonable alternative." (d) "People would be happier if sex experience before marriage were taken for granted in both men and women." (e) "I never attend a sexy show if I can avoid it." (f) "I believe women ought to have as much sexual freedom as men." (g) "I like to flirt." (h) "I like to talk about sex." The direction of change, of course, is that of the seniors' responding in the more "liberal" direction.

The interviews reveal a fairly uniform code of attitudes and behavior to which most students adhere. In response to the question "Have your ideas about sex changed at all during the college years?" 32 of the students reported that they had become more liberal, one reported that she had become more conservative, and seven reported no change. (The responses of nine subjects were not classifiable.) As Table 6 indicates, however, this increase in liberalization of attitude does not necessarily mean freedom of action. The personal sexual code of seniors may in essence be viewed as rather conservative. Being in love or being involved seriously with a man permits varying degrees of physical intimacy—but usually not intercourse. The standards by which the behavior of other students is judged are somewhat more liberal. Unless they behave promiscuously, students who have affairs are not condemned. Following are illustrative remarks by seniors:

> I've changed a lot. I'm a little more experienced. I don't condemn others who have sex relations, but it's not for me. I don't care what others do. I don't think I'd care much for someone who had no moral values sexually, but I detest professional virgins too.
>
> My ideas have changed, not my behavior. I still hold to my old beliefs, but I question them more. . . . Reading *Lady Chatterley's Lover* was a big step in changing my outlook.
>
> I used to think it was horrible not to be a virgin. I'm more realistic now. But I still think it would be nice for me to be a virgin.
>
> I'm a little more broad-minded about others, not myself.
>
> If you're very much in love, I think now it's all right to go ahead. I didn't used to. But I don't think *I* would.

Explanations of the reasons underlying the relatively conservative personal code—for example, responses to the question "What is the value of virginity?"—almost unanimously ignore abstract moral or ethical considerations. Only three students referred to religious precepts as important influences on their behavior.[7] External

[7] I do not mean that religious teaching or indoctrination is irrelevant to

authority is similarly rejected; only two students indicated that they feared that their parents might find out were they to have intercourse, while three others referred to the fear of shame were others to learn.[8] There was general agreement that virginity as an abstract virtue had little meaning. Only five students held that society would be damaged if the standard of virginity prior to marriage were to be widely transgressed. What these women had in mind chiefly were illegitimate children who would become society's responsibility. But the great majority of students drew the line at premarital intercourse for personal or interpersonal reasons.

These reasons were of a wide variety. Seven students indicated fears of pregnancy. Some spoke of feelings of "emotional upset," "guilt," or "loss of self-respect" that might be damaging to the relationship with the men involved. Lack of certainty about permanence of relationships was mentioned on occasion. For example, one of the students in the interview sample reported: "All of my roommates are virgins except for one. She's sorry now. She loved him, but he left her." A number of students wished to be virgins at the time of marriage because they thought that this was in some fashion important to the marriage. One student said that virginity seemed to her to be "sacred to a marriage." Another said she thought of it as a "gift to be brought to my husband." A similar sentiment expressed by one of the women was that it is "something only he can have."

Underlying many of the explanations seemed to be an unexpressed sense of caution or inhibition. Few of the students were disposed to argue with strong conviction the reasons they cited for maintaining the virginal state. Rather the explanations often seemed

---

the sexual feelings and behavior of students. I believe that students are profoundly influenced by a general sexual and moral ethos to which current religious doctrine and practice and the religious heritage of the past contribute. These influences tend to be imbibed osmotically or implicitly, however, rather than in concrete or explicit fashion.

[8] Similarly, a small group of students saw external value in retaining their virginity in that they considered virgins more eligible for marriage. All students in the interview sample were asked whether they thought that men preferred virgins for marriage partners. The majority thought that most men who were considering marriage did not care one way or the other.

to be mere vague surface manifestations of deep-lying and complex sentiments that were only dimly comprehended. Occasionally a hint of this emerged. One student said in response to the question about the value of virginity: "None. It's a stupid idea. Just a practical matter so you don't get pregnant." And then she added, "I guess I'm scared too." Another student, when queried about her views of premarital intercourse, reported: "When I was a freshman I thought sex was sacred to marriage. Now I think more of the risk. After so many years, naturally we do more than hold hands. But behind this is the old feeling. I couldn't have intercourse." And again in response to the question about the value of virginity: "It's difficult to assign a value. Perhaps it's irrational just one of those things." Similarly, several students reported that they set limits to their petting behavior, because they feared losing control.

As one would expect, the reasons presented by most of the non-virgins for transgressing the conventional sexual code had to do with "love's making right." Said one, with respect to the value of virginity: "If you're in love, it makes no difference." Said another: "There can't be any rules when you're engaged." And a third: "It would annoy me, if I couldn't show my love." Two of the members of the Uninhibited category expressed different sentiments, however. They were forthright in their views that physical attractiveness was sufficient warrant for sex relations, including intercourse. One said: "Sex is fun. Premarital relations are perfectly natural and healthy." And the other said: "Premarital relations are fine. I advise caution about pregnancy though."

It is reasonable to assume that variations in sexual behavior are functions of personality characteristics. All students are exposed to the predominant sexual code of the campus, but how they respond to this code is to some extent a function of internal dispositions. To test this assumption, relationships between the clinical scales of the Minnesota Multiphasic Personality Inventory[9] and the scales contained in the Vassar Attitude Inventory[10] (See Chapter 5)

[9] Hathaway and McKinley. Manual for the Minnesota Multiphasic Personality Inventory.

[10] Webster *et al. Research Manual for VC Attitude Inventory and VC Figure Preference Test.*

and the categories of sexual behavior presented in Table 6 were examined by means of analysis of variance. Analyses of variance were carried out separately for freshman and senior scores.

The only scale that is related significantly to the categories of sexual behavior for both freshmen and seniors is the Impulse Expression Scale—at the .01 level for freshmen and the .05 level for seniors. A rational clustering of the items of the scale after the fashion of the needs scheme developed by Henry Murray[11] yields the following needs as indicative of the traits possessed by high scorers on the Impulse Expression Scale: dominance, recognition, aggression, autonomy, acquisition, sex, exhibition, change, and excitancy. Needless to say, the order of mean scores for each category is such that higher scores are associated with greater sexual experience. The Mania Scale of the Minnesota Multiphasic Personality Inventory is related to sexual behavior at the .05 level—but for freshmen only. Subscales of the Mania Scale have been labeled Acceleration and Lability, Amorality, Ego Inflation, and Imperturbability.

The fact that seniors score significantly higher than freshmen on the Impulse Expression Scale suggests that greater sexual experience is associated with possession of qualities that increase with college attendance. Further, higher scores on the Impulse Expression Scale have been found to be significantly related to faculty nominations of students as "ideal."[12] (The interpretation of the term "ideal" was left to the faculty.) Apparently the characteristics that are measured by the Impulse Expression Scale are associated also with kinds of academic performance that are appealing to faculty members.

Other Studies of College Women

Even though the body of scientific research pertaining to the sexual attitudes and behavior of college women is small, the results

[11] Murray, Henry A. *Explorations in Personality.* New York: Oxford, 1938.

[12] Brown, Donald R. Personality, College Environment, and Academic Productivity. In Sanford (Ed.). *The American College.*

are consistent. Generally the studies show that fewer than 25 per cent of college women are not virgins. The Vassar studies just discussed yielded a figure of 22 per cent nonvirgins among seniors. Alfred Kinsey and Paul Gebhard[13] reported an incidence of 20 per cent nonvirgins among a national sample of college women aged twenty. It is likely that Kinsey's samples were biased in the direction of greater sexual experience. Kinsey recruited his subjects by asking for volunteers, and one would expect that people who volunteer to talk about their sex lives are likely to have more to talk about than those who do not.[14]

Winston Ehrmann[15] reported that 13 per cent of the women in a sample he studied indicated that they were not virgins. These were students, eighteen to twenty-two years of age, who were attending a large coeducational university. Ehrmann's lower figure may result from the presence of younger women in his samples. In addition, his subjects were students who were enrolled in a course called "Marriage and the Family"—one that the more sexually experienced undergraduates perhaps did not see fit to take. Thus the findings based on a national sample of volunteers, on students enrolled in a course in "Marriage and the Family" in a large coeducational university, and on a random sample of women at an eastern women's college coincide rather closely.

Of course, these results may not hold for all colleges and universities at which women are enrolled. Empirical inquiries of recent years into the characteristics of students who attend various colleges and universities demonstrate that there is much wisdom in the old saw "Birds of a feather flock together." When secondary school students are given a free choice among colleges to attend, they are likely to choose in accord with certain images of the colleges.[16] These images consist, in part, of reasonably accurate assessments of what the students at each are like. Students prefer to attend a col-

[13] Kinsey and Gebhard. *Sexual Behavior in the Human Female.*

[14] Maslow, Abraham H., and Sakoda, James M. Volunteer-Error in the Kinsey Study. *Journal of Abnormal and Social Psychology,* 1952, **47**, 252–267.

[15] Ehrmann. *Premarital Dating Behavior.*

[16] McConnell and Heist. The Diverse College Student Population.

lege at which a majority or at least many of their fellow students hold values similar to their own.

We have seen that the Impulse Expression Scale is a significant index of sexual behavior; women who obtain high scores in either the freshman or senior year are likely to be more "advanced" than low scorers in their sexual experience.[17] I know of several colleges at which students score very high on the Impulse Expression Scale. Among the women in attendance at these colleges, the proportions who have experienced intercourse are likely to be considerably higher than those reported earlier. And, of course, within larger institutions there are groups of students—friendship or residence groups—whose activities may differ widely from the prevailing standards. By and large, however, it may be assumed that some three-fourths of the women who attend the larger and the more prominent colleges and universities, public and private, are virgins.

Other studies likewise support the Vassar findings that, in the majority of cases, those women who do engage in intercourse do so in the context of a relationship of some seriousness with the man involved. They are engaged or going steady. Most premarital intercourse is confined to the future husband. Occasionally young women have several affairs involving intercourse before marriage, but these relationships are rarely limited to physical intimacy alone. Ehrmann reported the following as "probably the single most important empirical finding" of his research: "Female sexual expression is primarily and profoundly related to being in love and going steady."[18]

An implication of these remarks is that sexual promiscuity is rare among college women, and this is correct. Only a small percentage of college women engage in sex relations in a context in which there is little or no emotional intimacy. And this makes sense, if one reflects on the personal restraint and discipline required to gain entrance to a first-rate college or to remain in good standing after admittance. The disposition to gratify desires without delay or the inability to control sexual urges that characterizes a sexually

[17] See Chapter 7.
[18] Ehrmann. *Premarital Dating Behavior,* p. 269.

promiscuous woman is likely to be inversely related to academic or intellectual performance. Probably high schools contain larger proportions of promiscuous students than colleges do. Reporting on the differences between adolescent girls who plan to go to college and those who do not, Elizabeth Douvan and Carol Kaye[19] say: "The dream of college apparently serves as a substitute for more direct preoccupation with marriage: girls who do *not* plan to go to college are more explicit in their desire to marry, and have a more developed sense of their own sex role. They are more aware of and more frankly concerned with sexuality."

Although the majority of college women have not engaged in intercourse, most of them are by no means completely chaste in thought or act. Few students have had no sexual experience whatsoever or have confined their activities to kissing. Various degrees of petting are the norm. As one would anticipate on the basis of the context in which intercourse usually occurs, the extent of petting is very much a function of the degree of emotional intimacy with the man involved. Thus most seniors who have been seriously involved with men are likely to have gone fairly far in petting. This means that, by the time of graduation, a substantial number of the seniors who have not experienced intercourse, perhaps a majority on some campuses, have nevertheless participated in petting with genital involvement.

Kinsey and his associates report that at age twenty-five, 39 per cent of unmarried college alumnae are not virgins. This figure coincides with the results of my own studies. I have concluded that slightly more than 50 per cent of college women or alumnae will refuse to engage in premarital intercourse—save perhaps on the brink of marriage. At the other extreme are a small percentage who are promiscuous or uninhibited. In between, there is a sizable minority who are not uninhibited or promiscuous, but who are nonetheless disposed to enter into intercourse in the context of a serious relationship. The time at which these women first experience intercourse is often a function of their physical and social surroundings.

[19] Douvan, Elizabeth, and Kaye, Carol. Motivational Factors in College Entrance. In Sanford (Ed.). *The American College,* pp. 204–205.

Thus residential campus and dormitory housing for the majority of students are likely to delay intercourse until the postcollege years. As one young woman said to me, "Doing it in cars or motels just doesn't appeal to me." Where many students live in unsupervised housing, on the other hand—for example, in private apartments—those women who are inclined to engage in premarital intercourse are more likely to do so during the college years. This is not to say that unsupervised housing promotes promiscuity. Such housing does, however, make it more likely that couples who are engaged or seriously involved will have intercourse before graduation.

The sexual experience of most female freshmen at the time of college entrance is rather limited. All but a small percentage are virgins. Although the age at which dating starts these days is quite early (in metropolitan areas the onset of puberty and the beginning of dating are likely to coincide), relatively few girls who are college bound engage in more than kissing or light petting before the junior and senior years of high school. The freshman year of college is not likely to be marked by extensive sexual activity. Rather, college women gradually accelerate the pace of sexual involvement. When intercourse does occur, it is more likely to take place in the junior or senior year rather than earlier.

It appears that homosexual involvements and crushes have declined among college women since 1925. Certainly, personal reminiscences and literary descriptions of college campuses, particularly women's colleges, circa 1925, suggest an erotic ambiance that is seldom matched today. During the 1920's and earlier, for example, campus leaders in women's colleges occasionally made homosexuality something of a fad. In 1929, Katherine Davis reported that 19 per cent of her sample of women who had been at college prior to World War I had engaged with other women in ". . . intense relationships accompanied by mutual masturbation, contact of genital organs, or other physical expressions recognized as sexual in character." She concluded that homosexual activities ". . . are much more widespread than is generally suspected, or than most administrators are willing to admit."[20] Davis's sampling may have

[20] Davis, Katherine B. *Factors in the Sex Life of Twenty-Two Hundred Women.* New York: Harper, 1929, p. 245.

exaggerated these phemonena (her data were obtained by means of questionnaires which were sent out to a large sample of subjects, and only a small minority of the subjects who were canvassed responded), but it is likely nevertheless that her findings accurately reflect a prominent tendency of the times. In contrast, only 4 per cent of the women in college in the 1930's who responded to questionnaires sent out by Dorothy Bromley and Florence Britten[21] reported that they had engaged in homosexual practices. The proportions to be found among college women today are probably even lower.

Most college women seem to be content with their sexual status quo, although there are exceptions, of course. I have been impressed in the course of my research by the capacity of young women to carry on very well without any physical sexual activity whatsoever —including masturbation. As we shall see, this is true of some men as well. I am not sure what to make of this, for it does not fit very well into most psychological or biological theories of human development.

The Sexual Behavior and Attitudes of College Men

At the time of college entrance, as one would expect, many more men than women say that they have experienced intercourse —some 25 per cent of the men compared with a negligible figure for the women. By senior year the proportion of men who have engaged in premarital intercourse has risen to 50 per cent or perhaps slightly higher, versus about 25 per cent for women of the same age.

The views expressed by college men toward sexual matters are somewhat less conservative than those of college women. Consider the following summary of questionnaire replies of the freshman class at a men's college.[22] Two per cent of the class endorsed the view that their male contemporaries should be "as aggressive and have

21 Bromley, Dorothy D., and Britten, Florence H. *Youth and Sex*. New York: Harper, 1938.

22 MacNaughton, William S. *Comparative Profiles of Emergent Value Patterns in Undergraduate Life at Dartmouth*. Hanover, New Hampshire: Office of Student Counseling, Dartmouth College, 1966, p. 74.

as many sexual relations as possible, without a great deal of concern about who the partners in these affairs might be." Forty-two per cent agreed with the assertion that college-age men may well be expected "to have sexual relations with a number of young women, but with some discretion." Fourteen per cent of the class were of the opinion that men of college age should have sexual relations "only if both partners feel that they are in love at the time." Thirty-three per cent of the freshmen felt that college men "may well be expected to try to refrain from intercourse before marriage." Nine per cent felt that young men should "definitely avoid intercourse and situations which might lead to heavy petting and temptation." A negligible number, less than 1 per cent, believed that college men should "avoid physical contact with young women." These data suggest rather a cautious approach to sexual activities. Only 2 per cent of the men advocate what might be thought of as a promiscuous approach to sexual relations, and a majority of the class favor either continence before marriage or intercourse "only if both partners feel that they are in love." During the freshman year actual behavior tends to lag behind the expressed code. It is unlikely that all the students who expressed a rather liberal approach to sexual relations, 44 per cent, had engaged in intercourse at the time they answered the questionnaire.

As in the case of college women, the attitudes of college men toward sexual matters become more liberal during the college years. By the senior year, this same class responded as follows. Three per cent endorsed the view that their male contemporaries should be as aggressive and have as many affairs as possible. Sixty-six per cent agreed with the assertion that college-age men should "be free to have sexual relations with a number of young women, but with some discretion." Seventeen per cent of the class were of the opinion that college men should have sexual relations only if both partners were in love. Thirteen per cent of the seniors still felt that college men should "try to refrain from intercourse before marriage." And only 1 per cent felt that young men should "definitely avoid intercourse and situations which might lead to heavy petting and temptation."

In a poll which was carried out recently at a coeducational

college,[23] students were asked whether "premarital sexual relations should be condoned by society." Twenty-nine per cent of the women and 54 per cent of the men thought they should. Nineteen per cent of the women and 61 per cent of the men said that they had actually engaged in intercourse. (Seven per cent of the men, therefore, had engaged in sexual activities which in their view should not be condoned by society.) This discrepancy in outlook between college men and women makes for tension at times. It is not that most college men advocate libertinism. Many of them, however, consider it natural to have intercourse with a girl with whom they are going steady or to whom they are rather deeply attached, even though they may not be engaged or committed to the likelihood of marriage.

As in the case of college women, many of the college men who have had almost no sexual experience are little troubled by their abstinence. Consider the remarks of a hard-working predental student, whose sexual activity had been confined to kissing one girl several times:

> Naturally I think about girls sometimes, particularly on Saturday nights when a lot of the fellows are going out. I wish I had the time to go out more, but I'm just too busy during the school year. And in the summers I'm working very hard or camping in the wilderness on my vacation. There's a girl I see at church. I've walked home with her a few times after church. I would like to see more of her, but I just don't have the time now. I figure that I'll have more time for girls toward the end of dental school. Naturally I plan to get married as soon as I get settled in my practice.

This young man who could, with composure, put serious involvement with girls and sexual experience off to some indefinite point in the future is by no means unique. And while young men of this type are likely to be somewhat sedate, perhaps uninteresting, and lacking in complexity, sophistication, and spirit, there is no reason to think that they will not make satisfactory husbands and fathers

[23] What Students Think About Sex. *San Francisco Chronicle,* January 13, 1965, p. 17.

someday. Their existence is certainly a challenge to the view that sexual tension and conflict inevitably accompany development.

The sexual activities of about half the college men who have engaged in intercourse resemble those of the majority of college women in this category—that is, their sexual partners are women with whom they are involved in a relationship of some emotional intimacy. As a rule they have not had intercourse prior to college, and they have few affairs. Their sexual experience is sometimes confined to the one girl whom they eventually marry. Perhaps they have two or three affairs—rarely more. Prototypic of such behavior was the following young man. An outstanding student majoring in physical science, he was a varsity athlete and a graduate of a prominent prep school. In his junior year, he and his girlfriend, a student in the same school, began to have sex relations. It was the first such experience for both of them, although this young man reported of himself, "It was not for want of trying earlier." They were not engaged at the time of the study, but they were going steady, and there was a good chance they would marry. This young man thought that he would like to marry the girl, but he was reluctant to make a decision because of the uncertainties of his future. He was not yet sure of the field in which he would do graduate work, and he had, in addition, a hitch in the Marines awaiting him. He said, however, "I think I am in love with her."

There remains then a group of some 25 per cent of college men whose sexual activities differ substantially from those of the majority of the women in that they say that they are or have been fairly free. Usually these men have commenced intercourse during the high school years, and they have had intercourse with a number of girls, six or eight on the average. The attitudes toward women of most of these men are characterized by a double standard. There are sexual objects, and there are "good" girls toward whom one does not make sexual advances—or at least not really serious ones. In former eras, when social class differences were of more moment in American life, the sexual objects were likely to be girls of lower social status, usually town girls of working-class background who did not go on to college. Now, as social class lines have been somewhat blurred, the social class implications of this double standard are not so obvious, but some status differences based on class alignments still persist. Thus college men frequently seek sexual objects among high school girls of lower social status or among women at colleges of lower status. In some cases, the double standard is applied to women of equal social status. There are, for example, in one's own college, those girls who "do" and those who "do not."

Implied in this double standard is the notion that premarital sex is demeaning to the woman involved. As a consequence, such men cannot enjoy sex and true affection or intimacy in the same relationship—at least not prior to marriage, and often not even after marriage. One aspect or the other must predominate. A typical attitude of this kind, that of a senior man who had had sexual relations with some ten or twelve girls, none of them from his own college, was this: "About premarital sex . . . I've never seen any reasons for limits except for girls. They have to worry about their reputation and getting pregnant. If I really cared for a girl, I wouldn't push. A girl really close to me I'd like to be strict about her morals. With others I figure it's their lives."

The double standard also suggests a certain callousness or hardness toward the girls involved. Frequently the girls are "brief encounters" during a summer vacation. Often they are dates for "one night stands." The man is not concerned to know them well or to think about what happens to them after the relationship ends. Moreover, the double standard suggests an allegiance to a strict and rigid morality. There are the "good" girls whom one respects, to a considerable extent because they do not engage in premarital sex. And there are the "bad" girls whom one may desire physically; but they are immoral and are, therefore, undeserving of respect. There is no middle ground, so that a girl may be loved and respected, even though she is somewhat free sexually. In this sense the adherents of the double standard are rather old-fashioned traditional moralists. They are unsophisticated, and they are not very complicated people.

This is not to say that there are not a number of college men who are free sexually and who are generally more sophisticated. They do not condemn girls who have sex relations, and they do not consider premarital intercourse to be demeaning to the women involved. Those who decry the "sexual revolution on the campuses" usually have this kind of college man in mind. These men, supposedly, are the modern generation, free of the old traditional restraints. They know that they will not suffer eternal torment by fire and brimstone if they indulge in premarital sex, marijuana, alcohol, or what have you. Children of ethical, moral, and religious relativism, they seek sensation and gratification of impulse. Such college men exist, of course, but their contributions to the sex life of the campuses are usually exaggerated.

First, such men tend to be rather unsure of themselves. Often they are lacking in aggressiveness. Frequently they fear hurting others or being hurt themselves. For example, one young man majoring in literature came from a very sophisticated background. His parents had many literary connections, and he had spent several years in European schools. His parents had given him instruction in matters of contraception. He regarded premarital intercourse as "perfectly natural and healthy." But despite such "favorable" background, this young man had had intercourse with only one girl—and this a rather promiscuous girl who made herself readily available. He said he would like to expand the scope of his sexual activities, but added, "It does not seem to happen."

Or consider another young man who came from an academic family. His father was a professor in a prominent medical school. This student was much more sure of himself than the young man described above, and he had had a fair amount of experience in high school. In his freshman year he was of the opinion that "young people prior to marriage ought to be free to have sexual relations when they are attracted to each other physically." This young man later learned, to his regret, that he had hurt several girls in the course of having transient affairs with them, and in his junior year he was no longer sure of his views about premarital sex. He said at this time: "I don't think that I'm ready to say you ought to wait for marriage or until you're engaged. But I am a lot more cautious than I used to be. If you care for somebody, you don't want to hurt her."

Thus many of the college men who espouse the freest philosophy of sexual relations are rather conservative in actual practice.

They are inhibited by a concern for other people and a sensitivity to their feelings. The most active men sexually on a college campus are likely to be adherents of the double standard, not those students whose generalized liberal outlook on the world suggests a lack of regard for conventional restraints.

In contrast to the situation with college women, homosexuality is fairly prominent among college men. When one asks a psychiatrist who deals with college men what the array of problems is that his patients bring to him, homosexuality will invariably be listed along with depressions, study blocks, and suicidal impulses. The prevalence of homosexual activities among young men suggests caution in labeling them as homosexual. Many adolescents and youths who engage in homosexual activities engage in sexual activities with women concurrently or later on. Many of them marry and proceed to live conventionally masculine lives. Authorities advise that young people under the age of twenty-five or so who have displayed homosexual behavior should not be considered to have made any final choice. Nevertheless, many of the young men who engage in homosexual activities in the undergraduate years will not later find sexual satisfaction with women. Nor will they marry.

It is unclear whether homosexual activities among men have been increasing in recent years. Abram Kardiner, for example, says, ". . . male homosexuality has had a tremendous increase in the last three decades."[24] He adduces as evidence reports of psychotherapists to the effect that, while homosexuals had difficulty finding paramours 25 years ago, it is easy now. Kardiner also points to statistics of arrest. In England and Wales, for example, police arrests for homosexual offenses rose 400 or 500 per cent in the years following World War II.

It can be argued that these observations do not constitute valid evidence for a significant rise in the incidence of homosexuality. Rather they may indicate greater awareness of homosexuality and attention to it—an underground phenomenon becoming part of the public consciousness. Whatever the answer to this controversy, it is

[24] Kardiner, Abram. The Flight from Masculinity. In Ruitenbeek, Hendrik M. (Ed.). *The Problem of Homosexuality in Modern Society.* New York: Dutton, 1963, p. 18.

certain that homosexuality among men is not declining. It constitutes an important personal and social problem; and the greater frequency of homosexuality among educated men as compared with educated women indicates that, in modern western life, the barriers to social or psychological complementation of the biological male heritage are often formidable in the middle classes.

In summary, affairs among college students are usually confined to relationships of some seriousness. Frequently neither partner has had intercourse previously. On most campuses, female promiscuity is confined to a small percentage of women. Usually those men who are quite active sexually are involved either with this small group of college women who are very free or with high school girls or other women who are not attending college.

Except for some 25 per cent of the men, most entering freshmen are relatively inexperienced sexually. The majority of women and a substantial portion of the men express rather conservative views about sexual matters at the time of college entrance, tending to disapprove of premarital intercourse. Between college entrance and graduation, these conservative freshmen are likely to shift toward a more liberal outlook on sexual matters. Particularly among girls, however, personal conduct is likely to be more conservative than the sexual code of students as expressed in responses to psychological scales and questionnaires.

8

Sex and Society: Social and Historical Perspectives

The research reported in Chapter 7 indicates that the sexual behavior of college students is characterized more by restraint than by license. Yet this is not the image of college students that is conveyed by the popular press or by most critics and observers of the social scene. They suggest that radical changes in sexual activities and in outlook have occurred among college students in the last generation. Typical of such comments is this statement: "The contemporary mores of young people are so different from those which governed their parents' or teachers' lives that a common meeting ground between them scarcely exists."[1] Pitrim Sorokin[2] wrote of "proliferating promiscuity" and "growing sex addiction." In 1938, Lewis Terman[3] predicted the disappearance of the female unmar-

[1] Binger, Carl A. L. Emotional Disturbances among College Women. In Blaine, Graham B., Jr., and McArthur, Charles C. (Eds.). *Emotional Problems of the Student.* New York: Appleton-Century-Crofts, 1961.

[2] Sorokin, Pitrim A. *The American Sex Revolution.* Boston: Sargeant, 1956.

[3] Terman, Lewis M. *Psychological Factors in Marital Happiness.* New York: McGraw-Hill, 1938.

ried virgin by 1960. Yet if one examines the evidence, recent changes in sexual behavior and mores do not seem quite so sweeping.

The Impact of World War I

In the case of college men, it does not appear that things have changed much since the decade following World War I. The few studies of the pre-World War I era suggest that the proportion of men who had engaged in premarital intercourse was slightly higher than one-third. By 1930, this figure had risen to around 50 per cent. It may be that the proportion of college men who have experienced premarital intercourse is somewhat higher now. And perhaps higher percentages of the young men of today who have not had intercourse have had greater sexual experience short of intercourse. But in all, it appears that the situation has changed little since 1930.

Between 1915 and 1930 the percentage of college women who had experienced intercourse doubled or trebled, starting from a base of quite low incidence. In Katherine Davis's[4] study of the premarital sexual experience of a sample of women who had been in college in the early 1900's, 7 per cent stated that they had had intercourse prior to marriage. Dorothy Bromley and Florence Britten[5] reported that 25 per cent of a sample of women in college in the 1930's had engaged in premarital intercourse—a figure very close to the percentage of nonvirgins on today's campuses. These data suggest that the increase in premarital intercourse among college women that took place after World War I was stabilized by about 1930. If the proportion of nonvirgins among college women has risen since 1930, the increase has not been large. As one observer has pointed out, "A considerable degree of caution should be exercised in estimating the present and future rate of change in premarital sex behavior. Kinsey investigators particularly have emphasized the numerous factors in our culture making for stability. Despite the changes that have taken place since the turn of the

[4] Davis. *Factors in the Sex Life of Twenty-Two Hundred Women.*
[5] Bromley and Britten. *Youth and Sex.*

century, primarily in females, the tempo of change in sex behavior and mores is not a rapid one."[6]

To be sure, a revolution in freedom of relationships between men and women took place between 1910 and 1925. The casual and unsupervised dating behavior of today was unknown in American life before World War I. Along with casual dating went widespread acceptance of petting relationships, a change exemplified by F. Scott Fitzgerald's *This Side of Paradise*.[7] Although its popularity in the 1920's is regarded as evidence that the Jazz Age had replaced Victorian prudery, it is actually a surprisingly innocent book. Except for one incident involving a brush with the Mann Act, the sexual activities of the characters consist of kissing and petting—primarily kissing.

It may be that promiscuity has actually decreased on college campuses in recent decades. By promiscuity I mean sex relations in the absence of a relationship of some consequence. Consider the situation of college men in 1910 or 1920. The small proportion of nonvirgins among the college women of the day suggests that, in the great majority of cases, college women were not the sexual partners of the men. Most college men were having intercourse with town girls of lower social status or prostitutes. Nowadays, some 50 per cent of the college men who have intercourse do so in a context of a relationship of some seriousness with the woman involved.

Furthermore, while it is likely that on most campuses the percentages of promiscuous women have never been high, there is a good chance that they are lower now than in the decade prior to World War II. In the 1930's and earlier, college attendance was very definitely linked to social class. Except for a few colleges and universities, almost any student of reasonable intelligence who could afford to go to college was able to gain admittance. If a student was not concerned to get high grades, doing enough to get by academically was not difficult. On almost every campus there were a number of young women who were involved with little but proms and

[6] Rubin, Isadore. Sex and the College Student: A Bibliography of New Findings and Insights. *Journal of the National Association of Women Deans and Counselors,* 1963, **26,** 34–39.

[7] Fitzgerald, F. Scott. *This Side of Paradise.* New York: Scribner, 1948.

parties, and many young men whose interest included little more than women, drinking, and football. Nowadays, at least at those colleges and universities where academic standards are high, few men and women of this kind can be found.

There are exceptions, of course, particularly on certain college campuses where bohemian types abound, but by and large an inverse relationship is likely to exist between promiscuity and high academic standards. I think that this is even more true of men than of women. I know of a very prominent college at which the proportions of men and women who have engaged in intercourse are almost equal. The women are somewhat more experienced than is customary (although few are promiscuous), and the men are somewhat less so. I attribute the relative "backwardness" of the men to the high standards of the institution. The men who meet them are likely to be dutiful, controlled, and disciplined. Most of them have neither the time nor the inclination for sexual adventure.

The Decline of the Double Standard

Prior to World War I, in essentially Victorian times, women —that is, "ladies"—were not to enjoy sex. Sensuous enjoyment of all kinds was beneath them. It was, in fact, rather improper for a well-bred woman, circa 1900, to enjoy eating with gusto. Sex was something women endured for reasons of procreation.

All this began to change rapidly during and after World War I. Most college women do not now believe that physical passion and sensuous pleasure are instruments of the devil or signs of lack of breeding. The majority of college women have enjoyed the physical relations in which they have engaged, whatever their extent, and they are not reluctant to say so. Readers who are familiar with Oliver Goldsmith's *She Stoops to Conquer* will remember Mr. Marlow, the gentleman who is a perfect rake with barmaids but an utter incompetent with ladies of his own station. Miss Kate Hardcastle, the daughter of Squire Hardcastle, captures Mr. Marlow's fancy by disguising herself as a barmaid. At the end of the play, Miss Hardcastle and Mr. Marlow are wed; and in an epilogue, Mr. Marlow is assured of happiness by having, in the person of Miss Hardcastle, "a lady by day and a barmaid by night." There are more Kate Hardcastles around on college campuses these days than there were in times past.

Middle-class morality has not, of course, prescribed continence for young men, but only for women. And fidelity within marriage has been the duty of the wife rather than the husband. An occasional fling by a married man has had considerable social sanction, whereas for a married woman to have an affair has been a grave matter indeed. This view has infuriated feminists. Simone de Beauvoir,[8] for example, makes much of it.

The origins of the double standard for men and women are undoubtedly very complex, but the inhibitions of well-bred women have very likely contributed to it. If one assumed, as in Victorian days, that men had violent sexual appetites that had to be satiated, and if one regarded "ladies" as unfit sexual partners for such animal-like enterprises, then there had to be a class of women who were available for such purposes. As middle-class women have come increasingly to accept and even to enjoy sexual activities, the underpinnings of the double standard have been undermined. Nowadays only a minority of undergraduate women are willing to accord to their future husbands the privilege of an occasional extramarital adventure.[9] I suspect that a generation ago this proportion would have been much higher.

In the past two generations, the sexual behavior of college women has become more like that of college men. Women have become much more frank in acceptance of sexuality within themselves, and their sexual behavior has become freer. Various studies of the interests of men and women[10] demonstrate that, with increasing education, the interests of men and women become more alike. Thus, just as the sexual behavior of women has moved closer to that of men, so has the behavior of men come to resemble that of women. In comparison with the era prior to 1930, fewer men now

[8] De Beauvoir, Simone. *The Second Sex.* New York: Knopf, 1953.

[9] Freedman, Mervin B. The Role of the Educated Woman: An Empirical Study of the Attitudes of a Group of College Women. *The Journal of College Student Personnel,* 1965, **6**, 145–155.

[10] Strong, Edward K., Jr. *Change of Interests with Age; Vocational Interests of Men and Women.*

find it necessary to divorce sex from love and affection. Sex may now be had, as it were, with girls they love and respect.

Sex Education and Contraceptives

It is rare these days to encounter a college student who is unacquainted with the biology of sex and reproduction. Interview studies[11] indicate that young people acquire this knowledge fairly early, the intellectual enlightenment of American society now being such that the majority of young people in the middle classes are well prepared for the biological changes of puberty. They receive this information from parents, from school authorities, from literature, and from their peers.

This phenomenon represents a considerable change in American life. I have interviewed college alumnae born about 1910 who reported that they had been completely bewildered by their physiological changes in early adolescence, and that even in the college years, they knew almost nothing of the biology of sex and reproduction. Such women were the heirs of the Victorian repression and suppression that have gone by the board—at least intellectually. I am reminded of a lecture I once heard by the late Siegfried Bernfeld, a psychoanalyst who was a younger contemporary of Freud in Europe. Bernfeld was saying that it was almost impossible for modern young people to appreciate the total blotting out of sex that characterized a Victorian upbringing. "It," that is, sex, "just did not exist," he said.

There is one conspicuous exception to this new sophistication, however, and that is knowledge of contraceptives. It is difficult to get accurate information on this subject; I have been unable to find any systematic studies on knowledge of contraceptive techniques or use of contraceptives by college students. Students who are rather experienced sexually, mostly men, of course, know a good deal about the subject. But a great many other students know very little. Presumably, most programs of sexual education that are carried on in school omit consideration of contraceptive techniques. Very likely this happens because there is concern lest attention to them

[11] See Chapter 7.

be construed as some kind of encouragement of their use. Probably similar doubts plus elements of embarrassment act to prevent parents from imparting such knowledge.

As a consequence, many college students who are having intercourse, particularly for the first time, are not using contraceptives. In some cases students are explicit about their reasons for not taking contraceptive precautions: The use of contraceptives would be too mechanical; contraceptives require that an individual think beforehand about what he is likely to do, that he plan his actions; and all this would rob sexual relations of some of the charm of spontaneity.

More often, students can give no reason for the failure to use contraceptives. As they describe things, sex relations just happen—quite spontaneously, without any explicit plan; and besides, they add, they do not know much about contraceptives. These attitudes convey a feeling that many students do not really wish to face the issues involved for them in having sex relations. It may be more romantic for sexual relations simply to develop spontaneously, but it is often easier morally as well. One simply lets things happen. Of course, sometimes a pregnancy occurs. When one hears of young women who are engaging in intercourse without taking contraceptive precautions, it is hard to escape the thought that they may be flirting with pregnancy as a punishment for unconscious feelings of guilt. It may be that, on one occasion, a couple is caught up in the sweep of passions, and caution is thrown to the winds. Repeated relations without contraceptives are, however, much harder to comprehend.

The Puritan Heritage

Despite an appearance of worldliness and sophistication, most college students are conservative and cautious. The Puritan heritage has by no means passed from the American scene, despite surface manifestations to the contrary and despite various statements that American family life and middle-class life in general are coming apart at the seams. It is true that, as compared with pre-World War I days, belief in a fixed set of morals and ethics—as, for example, a code of behavior based on religious dogma—has waned.

Thus few college students can propound with any conviction ethical arguments for sexual abstinence or continence. Accordingly, they are loath to condemn the behavior of other people. This does not mean, however, that the feelings that underlie these fixed convictions have disappeared. Puritan sentiments, that is, inhibition of appetites and instincts, are still a strong feature of American middle-class life; they have been and are still being passed on from generation to generation. Consequently, most college students behave conventionally even though they may not adhere to any explicit moral code.

These underlying feelings of caution, control, and inhibition are often overlooked by individuals who speak of the "contraceptive revolution," or by people who question whether a social ethic will restrain youth in the same way as controls based on authority. Sexual behavior, apparently, is assumed to be entirely a rational or practical matter. If birth control pills are readily available, they reason, college women will now act with the abandon that only fear of pregnancy curbed. Students whose sexual desires have been restrained by a system of moral principles which they now question will perforce proceed to indulge themselves. Similarly, advocates of such practices as "companionate marriage" or premarital intercourse to determine "compatibility" seem to regard these activities as simple intellectual enterprises. They are logical recommendations. Why then should people not accept them?

I am arguing, in short, that the essential conservatism of the American middle class has been overlooked and that no sexual revolution is currently taking place on American campuses. Such changes as have taken place since World War I are not great, and the changes occurring now seem to me to be evolutionary rather than revolutionary. We have already seen in the preceding chapter that interview studies of modern college students, both men and women, bear out this contention. I should like to turn now to evidence from another source—the scrutiny of social movements and social institutions.

Early Marriage

Early marriage among college students and young alumni began abruptly with the war classes of 1941 to 1945. As of 1956, one out of every four students in college was married. If older college students were omitted from consideration, leaving only those of more typical college age, that is, eighteen to twenty-four, the figure dropped to about one in six, still a high proportion of married students. The age of marriage among young people in the United States, which was declining steadily in the years after World War II, now seems to have leveled off. There is, however, no evidence that it is rising. In short, a substantial number of undergraduate students are married, and within three or four years after graduation the great majority of alumni are married.

Now I fail to see the connection between "proliferating promiscuity" and early marriage. My view of things would be that young people who were having a very good time indulging in sexual adventure and exploration would be in no hurry to marry. Of course, it could be argued that young people enter upon marriage these days in very tentative fashion. Many of them will be involved in adulterous affairs, if not in "mate-swapping" clubs, and they will sue for divorce as soon as someone else catches their fancy. Marriage is simply a continuation of loose sexual morality.

This notion does not accord with my perception of things. I have studied a number of college alumnae of various ages by means of tests, questionnaires, and interviews, and by and large, I have been impressed by the stability and general conventionality of their lives. Divorce among college-educated people is less frequent than among the population at large. Since rates of divorce are correlated with age of marriage—the earlier the marriage, the greater the likelihood of divorce—the frequency of divorce among college alumni rose, beginning in 1941, with the trend toward earlier marriage. The divorce rate among college-educated people has remained fairly constant since the early 1940's, however. A study of divorce statistics for the last several decades provides no evidence that marriages among college graduates are becoming increasingly unstable or that the family lives of these people are disintegrating.

The coincidence of the abrupt drop in age of marriage with the outbreak of World War II suggests an obvious relationship. In response to the uncertainties and anxieties of wartime, young people looked to marriage for some kind of security. (This was very different from the effect of World War I on the United States, which was to loosen conventional ties.) The custom of early marriage which began with World War II has continued through the Cold War period, and has likely been reinforced by our military involvements in Korea and Vietnam.

To some extent, early marriage also reflects affluence. In the Depression years of the 1930's, for example, young people often had to wait for years before they could afford to marry. Frequently, engaged couples faced a choice between marrying immediately and moving in with parents, or postponing marriage for some indefinite period, until they could afford a place of their own. At that time, most undergraduates never even thought of marrying during college. Now, as befits the wealthiest nation, the United States has the lowest marriage age of any industrialized society; and the age of marriage is declining in other countries of the western world as well.

Affluence and wartime stresses do not completely explain early marriage, however. Early marriage has deeper psychological and social roots. It represents a solution to the conflict between sexual desire and the strictures of conscience, particularly for women. Contemporary college women are unwilling to postpone sexual gratification for a long time or to forego it completely. Prior to World War II, college-educated women married at a considerably later age than they do now, and a good many did not marry at all. This was particularly true of women who obtained advanced degrees. Nowadays women with graduate degrees are marrying at an increasing rate.[12] This is probably the biggest change in the marriage patterns of today's educated women as compared with those of the era prior to 1940.

Certain critics of the social scene have recently been exhorting educated women not to marry as young as they do. Early marriage, it is asserted, frequently hampers or limits the intellectual and social development of women. There is considerable validity in this argument. Yet in the absence of social support for an ethic of greater

[12] McBride, Katherine. Alumnae—Bryn Mawr College. *Case Book—Education Beyond the High School.* Washington, D.C.: United States Office of Education, 1958.

sexual freedom among young middle-class women, marriage is not likely to be deferred for long.

In this discussion of early marriage I have been addressing myself primarily to the motivations and circumstances of the women involved. This is the usual approach. Young women are frequently portrayed as having nothing on their minds but marriage. As they approach a suitable age, twenty-one or so, the greater part of their waking hours are thought to be devoted to spinning a web in which to ensnare a man. (Presumably, when they are not awake, the scenarios of their dreams are based on the same themes.) This view of things, as Nevitt Sanford has pointed out,[13] overlooks the contributions of the young men involved.

Very frequently college men's needs for intimacy are neglected. By and large, men have to keep up a bolder front than do women; they have to act as if they were in control of everything. Rarely can men admit to one another that they need help and comfort. Now it often happens that, as a young man becomes involved with a woman, he finds that he can relax—he can be himself, warts and all—and still be accepted, perhaps loved. To many a man, a relation of intimacy with a woman is like catnip to a cat. He becomes addicted to it. So it is that many a marriage among undergraduates or young alumni is powered by the needs of the man for intimacy and security.

The needs of young women and men to find security in marriage, children, and a home cannot be overemphasized. Such needs far outweigh impulses toward promiscuous sexual behavior. College youth are attempting to find or to establish in a marriage the security that is not to be found elsewhere in this uncertain age. We live from day to day with a military conflict that may suddenly erupt into a major war. In highly mobile industrial societies, communities—in the sense in which they existed in the nineteenth century and earlier, that is, places in which people knew each other and could count on one another—are rapidly disappearing. The comfort of the Christian myth, the simple faith that God's will was

[13] Sanford, Nevitt. Developmental Studies of the Entering Freshman. In Sanford (Ed.). *The American College.*

being done and that this earthly existence was but a prelude to a supernal hereafter, began to wane with Newtonian science and the relativism that was introduced by the religious wars of the sixteenth century.

I believe that college students are groping toward a new ethic that will replace the Calvinist ethic of individualism, hard work, and competition with an ethic of social concern that emphasizes love and human relationships.[14] To some extent, this represents a return to the Christianity of Jesus, for whom mercy and charity were the supreme virtues. I believe that the sexual behavior and attitudes of most college students, and the phenomenon of early marriage, represent a reaction against the depersonalization of modern life. Students are attempting to preserve human intimacy and the institution of the family.

Feminism and Women's Role

Changes in the role and status of women in a society and changes in sexual mores and outlook tend to run parallel. Just as Edna St. Vincent Millay in 1925 represented a very different kind of young woman from the proper young lady of 1910, so had the sexual customs of Miss Millay's times departed from those of the pre-World War I era. Women of Elizabethan times, for example, Queen Elizabeth I herself or the young Protestant martyr Lady Jane Grey, were separated from medieval times by only a few generations, but they were hardly medieval women—either in demeanor or in erudition. The lustiness, bawdiness, general freedom, and occasional licentiousness of the Elizabethan era indicated a great change in ethos. Renaissance Italy differed in similar fashion from medieval Italy.

I have argued that sexual behavior and mores have not changed radically since 1930, and this is true of the status of women as well. The early feminists, with the exception of Mary Wollstonecraft in England, tended to be rigid moralists on sexual matters. They wanted suffrage for women, access to the same educa-

[14] See Chapter 13.

tional and employment opportunities as men, and a just measure of human dignity. But they did not advocate that women be afforded the sexual freedoms of men. In the decade after World War I, however, feminism, at least for many of its adherents, implied a full measure of sexual freedom and the abandonment of the double standard. If men could indulge in premarital sex relations or in extramarital affairs, then so could women.

The economics of the welfare state, as it began to take shape after World War I, contributed to this point of view. In the late 1920's Bertrand Russell,[15] for example, argued that the emergence of the state as an important agency in the care of children considerably undermined the traditional patriarchal family. Since the father was no longer the sole barrier against starvation or the poorhouse for his wife and offspring, his tyranny over his wife could no longer be quite so effectively maintained. One facet of this tyranny was, of course, the double standard of sexual morality. Lord Russell went on to advocate that the sexual code of the western world be amended so as to permit both sexes the freedom of premarital and extramarital intercourse—to be practiced with some judiciousness, of course.

The doctrine of equality between the sexes, as it is propounded today, does not include advocacy of sexual permissiveness for either sex—at least, not after marriage. Most college-educated women feel that extramarital affairs should not be condoned in either husband or wife. And while there is some disposition to grant young men greater freedom prior to marriage, the double standard is actually breaking down here as well.

The disposition on the part of educated women to demand fidelity of men rather than sexual freedom for themselves suggests a conservatism, an attempt to preserve the traditional institution of home and family. Interview studies of college women indicate a slight preference that the husband be the dominant figure in making major decisions—"sixty-forty," as one student put it. The inter-

[15] Russell, Bertrand. *Marriage and Morals.* New York: H. Liveright, 1929.

views also reveal some reluctance on the part of women to assume leadership in various professions or fields except for those which possess considerable feminine connotation—for example, social work. They are likely to retreat from any exceptional accomplishment which may threaten the status or security of men. Consider the remarks of an excellent student who planned an ambitious career: "A boy wants a girl to be independent, but not a threat in his work." Another, the recipient of a fellowship for graduate study, said: "Equality is hard on a man. He may believe in liberated women, but it is hard emotionally." I suggest that educated women are reluctant to assert themselves for fear that the none-too-secure sex identities of middle-class men will thereby be rendered even more precarious. All in all, as I see it, most women today are striving to maintain the integrity of the family and, at least to some extent, the continuity of traditional sex roles.

I have qualified the preceding statement by adding "at least to some extent," because I hardly wish to suggest that college women want to return to the role of the submissive nineteenth-century wife and mother. Most educated women are not inclined to surrender the equality of station and outlook they have won. And it is this sense of equality that serves, among women, as a very strong barrier to sex relations in the absence of love. The chances are that a woman who gives of herself in such a relationship has a rather low opinion of herself. She may feel inferior because she is of lower class status than the man; she may feel that she has nothing to give a man of higher social station except her body. Sometimes, for psychological reasons, women of middle or high social position feel the very same way—for example, the young woman I mentioned in Chapter 7 who feared that men "valued" her "only for my body." In one interview, she described very poignantly how she felt so awkward and anxious in the company of men that she did not know what to do except go to bed with them. As she put it, "This seems to be the only thing I have to give them."

Equality of status between the sexes, or at least a considerable measure of it, has long been a feature of American life. Alexis de Tocqueville was very much struck by it in his American travels, and in *Democracy in America*[16] he connects the "great regularity of morals" he observed in America with this principle of equality.

> . . . the equality of conditions has swept away all the imaginary or the real barriers which separated man from woman. No girl then believes that she cannot become the wife of the man who loves her; and this renders all breaches of morality before marriage uncommon; for, whatever be the credulity of the passions, a woman will hardly be able to persuade herself that she is beloved, when her lover is perfectly free to marry her and does not.[17]

Peer Influence on Sexual Behavior and Attitudes

To argue, as I have, that most college students are rather conventional in sexual attitudes and behavior implies that these students have a fair degree of internal control over sexual desires and impulses. Surely the freedom that most college students have is such that they could readily behave much less conservatively than they do. Middle-class girls have a great deal of freedom in matters of dating from an early age. I believe that parents, particularly mothers, can tender this freedom to their daughters without misgiving because they sense that the girls will behave with restraint even in the absence of external controls.

As Chapter 4 indicates, in only a minority of cases are the home lives of college women characterized by strong resentment of parental standards and by intense antagonism between them and other family members. Most college women describe fairly placid home lives. But although they have incorporated parental values and mores, college women are, nonetheless, considerably influenced by their peers.

As I have written elsewhere, ". . . the scholastic and academic aims and processes of the College are in large measure transmitted

[16] De Tocqueville, Alexis. *Democracy in America.* New York: The Century Co., 1898.

[17] De Tocqueville. *Democracy in America,* Vol. 2, pp. 250–251.

to incoming students or mediated for them by the predominant student culture."[18] I know of a women's college where, during one year, an extraordinary number of freshmen in one residence hall became pregnant. Study of the situation revealed that this residence hall contained an unusually large number of juniors and seniors who were rather free sexually. These upperclassmen had conveyed to the freshmen something of their cavalier spirit toward sexual matters, on which the freshmen proceeded to act. Their inexperience and lack of knowledge were such that they did not take proper precautions.

Such peer pressures are probably stronger on men, among whom the range of sexual attitudes and behavior is somewhat greater and whose sexuality is rather more external. A familiar figure is the freshman man who thinks that there is something wrong with him because he has had little or no sexual experience. He listens to the talk around him about how all the other men are "making out." Often he is really not ready for sexual experience, and yet he feels that he must try in order to prove to his friends and to himself that he is really a man. In circumstances in which a young man is very concerned about his adequacy, he is likely to be rather inadequate.

When I worked as a psychotherapist in a student health service, I had as a patient a student who was in the depths of despair because of his sexual shortcomings. He was convinced that he was impotent because on the one occasion when he had attempted to have intercourse he had been impotent. This occasion would have taxed the manhood of Agent 007. It occurred when this young man was eighteen and was serving overseas in the army. He had been induced by comradely pressure to queue up in a line of men who were being entertained by a prostitute. This prostitute was receiving her customers on the earthen floor of a little hut. As the situation was described to me, the only thing conducive to having sexual intercourse was that it was summer. There was, at least, no frost on the ground.

[18] Freedman, Mervin B. The Passage through College. In Sanford (Ed.). Personality Development during the College Years, p. 14.

Most college men are not so naïve, but a good many are. And so are a good many women. This, of course, is particularly true of the freshmen. And the naïveté of many freshmen has certain implications, I believe, for the regulation of the lives of students in residential colleges. The unsophisticated state of many students who are entering college calls for a certain degree of institutional structure during the first year or perhaps two years. The freshman and sophomore years are a time of experimentation for most students. I should think that a college ought not to discourage such experimentation; but until the time when the majority of students have acquired an appropriate degree of control, some support from the institution would seem appropriate.

Some statistics on drinking from a men's college[19] illustrate the point I am making here. A questionnaire was submitted on three occasions—at the end of the freshman, the sophomore, and the senior years—to the members of a recent graduating class. The results indicated that the percentage of students who drank increased during the college years. For example, 64 per cent of the freshmen, 80 per cent of the sophomores, and 85 per cent of the seniors reported that they drank spirits. The questionnaire also asked the question: "As a result of drinking, how many times have you passed out?" Fourteen per cent of the freshmen versus 5 per cent of the seniors reported that they had passed out at least once during the previous year. In addition, the fact that few freshmen reported passing out from drinking prior to college indicates that many men are initiated into overindulgence on first coming to college. It seems reasonable to presume that statistics for sexual behavior would reveal similar trends.

Just as students find support in one another for resisting the requirements of authority, many students need aid, at least temporarily, in opposing the demands of their peers. William Blake, that remarkable spokesman for social freedom and freedom of the spirit, recognized that true sexual fulfillment comes from an inno-

[19] Birney, Robert C., Coplin, Haskell R., and Grose, Robert F. *The Class of 1959 at Amherst College*. Amherst, Mass.: Committee on Guidance and Counseling, 1960, pp. 68–69.

cence that is untrammeled by false experience. He saw false experience in his own time as residing in the institutions of society:[20]

> The harvest shall flourish in wintry weather
> When two virginities meet together:
> The King and the Priest must be tied in a tether
> Before two virgins can meet together.

In an age in which the forces of tradition were strong, the enemies of innocence were the state, which he called the "beast," and its "whore," which was his term for the established church. Nowadays, we must cry out as well against the tyranny of peer opinion.

Optimal Sexual Development

Those college seniors who seem the "best off" sexually—that is, those who, regardless of actual experience, seem to have a considerable capacity for warmth, intimacy, and bodily enjoyment and, at the same time, have an appropriate amount of control over their sexual behavior—are not likely to have been sexually precocious. Students who have commenced sexual intercourse on a regular basis fairly early in the secondary school years usually do not present a favorable picture when they are seniors in college. The girls often have deep-lying personality difficulty. They lack basic integrity or self-respect; they suffer from confusions of sexual identity; and they are incapable of sustaining intimate relationships with men over long periods. The men are often rather insensitive and shallow. Frequently they reveal considerable underlying homosexual disposition in their concern to impress their male friends with their sexual prowess. Both men and women convey the impression of individuals who are not likely to travel very far along the paths of intellectual or personal development. Many students who convey the impression that they are going a long way in terms of personality development seem to display instead a slow and gradual unfolding of sexual interests and behavior.[21]

[20] Blake, William. Merlin's Prophecy. In Sampson (Ed.). *William Blake's Poetical Works,* p. 195.

[21] Harvey Peskin's studies of early and late maturation in pubertal boys

These observations have implications for educators, parents, and other authorities who are concerned with the instruction of youth. A degree of cautiousness or naïveté about sexual matters in childhood and early adolescence is likely to do no harm and may, in fact, be all to the good. I am hardly advocating a return to the repressiveness and authoritarianism that characterized many of the nineteenth-century practices of child-rearing. Even though the sexual development of a young person be slow, there should be a capacity for eventual incorporation of sexual impulses into the personality. On the other hand, there is more than a suggestion that precocious participation in sexual activities does not augur well for future development—at least not in American society. This probably holds for drinking practices as well. Whether precocious involvement is an indication of some defects of control or integration or whether it actually has deleterious effects on the development of such control or integration is an enigma. Very likely, an interplay of both factors is at work.

Sexuality and the Future

"Science," says J. Bronowski, "will create values . . . and discover virtues when it looks into man; when it explores what makes him man and not an animal, and what makes his societies human and not animal packs."[22] I have been writing about sexual attitudes and behavior. Our real concern, however, is the meaning of love and the reconciliation of biological inheritance with human ideals. The real questions and issues have to do with the import of these empirical findings for the future conduct of our lives and for the kind of society we want to create.

In the near future, western society, and eventually the whole world, will be confronted with the question of the meaning of life in a godless world—or at least in a world in which God's ways are revealed to man only obscurely. This is hardly a new question, but

---

lend some support to this outlook. See Pubertal Onset and Ego Functioning: A Psychoanalytic Approach. *Journal of Abnormal Psychology* (in press).

[22] Bronowski. *The Common Sense of Science,* pp. 147–148.

it will soon assume an awesome immediacy. Throughout most of the Christian era, people have been sustained by their faith. This faith waned with the advent of the Industrial Revolution, but the struggle to maintain life has gone on. Most people, at least men, have been defined socially by the work they do. Most learning or education, formal and informal, has been in the service of preparing people for work roles. For most people and most families, work has been the pivot upon which existence has rotated.

In the future, as machines take over most of the burdens of production, traditional work will be of much less importance. Life will be characterized by much more leisure than people have now—enforced leisure, perhaps. How will people define themselves? What will give life meaning? I am not suggesting that the study of sexuality will answer questions like this, but it may provide some very good leads.

Puritanism and the Industrial Revolution went hand in hand. Puritanism did not bring about the Industrial Revolution, but Puritan asperity, discipline, and suppression of the instincts undoubtedly contributed to the work ethic necessary to accomplish industrialization. The more unfortunate consequences of these social trends are delineated in Henry Murray's statement concerning the oppression of "all joyous originations in art, in religion, in life."[23] As the Industrial Revolution draws to an end, as people are no longer defined by the work they do and are not required to work long hours or to work hard, society is offered the prospect of recapturing the joyous originations of which Murray speaks.

This means, among other things, a resurgence of the impulse life, of instincts or biology. Our society needs a suffusion of eroticism, of spontaneity, of joie de vivre. This is sexual, although not sexual in a narrow sense. Matthew Arnold described the governing idea of ancient Greek civilization as spontaneity of consciousness. We need more of this in our lives. "The gospels of love and mercy set forth in the major religions are not being challenged here but rather that part of religion which attempts to persuade man to

[23] See Chapter 2.

renounce the joys of this world for those of the world to come."[24] A biologist, a Nobel laureate, was asked recently whether the consumption of alcohol should be discouraged. He responded not on biological grounds, but rather on the basis of psychological or social concerns. "No," he said. "People need more simple pleasures in their lives." Of these simple pleasures, sex is perhaps foremost.

We are currently seeing some evidence of the revival of eros in our culture. In learned society there is the writing of men like Norman Brown,[25] Herbert Marcuse,[26] and Paul Goodman.[27] Joseph Katz and Nevitt Sanford[28] have suggested to college educators that the true ally of the teacher is the impulse life of students, not the conscience; that the best scholarship arises out of a sense of passionate involvement on the part of students, not out of a sense of duty or fear of punishment or disapproval. We see the decline of prudery in journalism, films, and books.[29] I think the best evidence for the resurgence of eroticism, however, is the sexual behavior of college youth, as I have described it—the behavior of college women, in particular.

The sexual attitudes and behavior of college women of the past several decades show considerable decline in constrictedness and prudery as compared with former eras. What I find especially appealing is their attempt to weld this revived eroticism to social affirmation, to love. As I see it, the real threats to a humane society and to a full life for the individual come from anomie[30] and de-

[24] Barach, Alvan L. Extramedical Influence of the Physician. *Journal of the American Medical Association,* 1962, **181,** 393.

[25] Brown, Norman O. *Life Against Death.* Middletown, Connecticut: Wesleyan University Press, 1959.

[26] Marcuse, Herbert. *Eros and Civilization.* Boston: Beacon Press, 1955.

[27] Goodman, Paul. *Compulsory Mis-Education.* New York: Horizon Press, 1964.

[28] Katz and Sanford. The Curriculum in the Perspective of the Theory of Personality Development.

[29] Unfortunately, sexuality in American culture frequently has more to do with the values of the market place than with eroticism. The use of pretty girls for the purpose of selling things is the foremost example.

[30] The concept of "anomie" was developed by Emile Durkheim to describe the collapse of traditional norms and values in a society.

personalization. Eroticism—defined as "the love life in any or all of its physical or psychical manifestations"[31]—is the best counter I can think of to this threat.

What is needed among youth today is more eroticism rather than more obeisance to conventional repressive morality. We need more love, more affection, more consideration, more respect for human dignity. This is the direction in which students are going, I think, as evidenced by their involvement in social phenomena like the Peace Corps and the civil rights movement. This form of eroticism in the broadest sense is not a threat to civilized society, but a reaffirmation of it.

Undoubtedly, life will in many ways become uglier and more difficult in the near future. International conflict, as in Vietnam, may be intensified. There will be more pollution in the city air and more violence in the streets. Islands of rural peace and beauty will become scarcer. Various computer experts say that the more closely the human being works with the computer, the more likely he is to resemble it in his ways of thinking. In the face of anomie, ugliness, and depersonalization, many young people are likely to reject human contact and social affirmation. Thus I am not nearly so troubled by the prospect of sexual promiscuity on college campuses as I am by the prospect of a large number of the more intelligent and sensitive college students withdrawing from participation in society.

A long time ago I read a passage which has lingered on in my mind:

> It seems possible that . . . the tendency . . . that has above all persisted and grown in the modern world . . . [has] pointed forward to a skepticism not only of the government of the world by an ultimate and supreme Will and Intelligence, but to a skepticism of all values. It may be that this is the direction in which modern thought, as a whole, is moving. . . . It may be that as man advances in phenomenal knowledge he loses belief in values and even in the possibility of knowing. May we look forward to a time when man will be able to do what he will and

[31] *Webster's New International Dictionary of the English Language*, Second Edition, Unabridged. Springfield, Mass.: G. & C. Merriam Co., 1953, p. 869.

> have no rational motive for doing anything? Then he will have achieved his sword of sharpness and his cap of invisibility, his magic carpet and Aladdin's lamp and find no reason for using them. For complete skepticism must needs destroy the basis of even the crudest utilitarianism. It may be that, in the long run, even desire will fail.[32]

As I see it, the only real obstacle to the fulfillment of this dire prophecy is reaffirmation of biology, of instinctual living—to which sexuality is the key. But instinct must be reconciled with ideals. We must have sexuality in the context of true human encounter.

[32] Allen, John W. *A History of Political Thought in the Sixteenth Century*. London: Methuen, 1941, p. 516.

IV

THE EDUCATION OF WOMEN

9

The Role of the Educated Woman: Attitudes of Vassar Students

Concern with the position or status of women as an explicit social issue goes back about 100 years. Alexis de Tocqueville, for example, devoted considerable attention to the state of American women in *Democracy in America,*[1] and John Stuart Mill's essay "The Subjection of Women"[2] appeared in 1869. In the latter half of the nineteenth century and in the early decades of the twentieth century, drama and fiction reflected the increasing importance of this topic. Ibsen's *A Doll's House*[3] and Virginia Woolf's *A Room of One's Own*[4] and *Three Guineas*[5] are good examples.

Since World War II, the role of educated women in our society has fallen within the purview of the behavioral scientists. To

[1] De Tocqueville. *Democracy in America.*

[2] Mill, John Stuart. The Subjection of Women. In *Three Essays by John Stuart Mill.* London: Oxford University Press, 1912.

[3] Ibsen, Henrik. *A Doll's House.* New York: Lovell, 1889.

[4] Woolf, Virginia. *A Room of One's Own.* London: Hogarth, 1935.

[5] Woolf, Virginia. *Three Guineas.* New York: Harcourt, Brace, 1938.

cite but a few, there are Marie Jahoda and Joan Havel,[6] Florence Kluckhohn,[7] Mirra Komarovsky,[8] Margaret Mead,[9] Mabel Newcomer,[10] David Riesman,[11] Nevitt Sanford,[12] and Anna-Liisa Sysiharju.[13] One may add the work of current literary or journalistic figures such as Simone de Beauvoir,[14] Betty Friedan,[15] and Sonya Rudikoff.[16]

This chapter reports the results of empirical studies of the attitudes of a group of college women to the various activities that have been subsumed under the term "women's role." Their attitudes toward careers, marriage, the ideal position of women in society, and similar topics were explored. Most of the findings are based on conversations with 49 Vassar seniors who were interviewed several times a year beginning in their freshman year.[17] The following kinds of questions were asked: "What do you criticize in a woman? What significant contributions are women making to American life? Are

[6] Jahoda, Marie, and Havel, Joan. Psychological Problems of Women in Different Social Roles. *Educational Record,* 1955, **36,** 325–335.

[7] Kluckhohn, Florence. American Women and American Values. In Bryson, L. (Ed.). *Facing the Future's Risks.* New York: Harper Bros., 1952.

[8] Komarovsky, Mirra. Cultural Contradictions and Sex Roles. *American Journal of Sociology,* 1946, **51,** 184–189; Functional Analysis of Sex Roles. *American Sociological Review,* 1950, **15,** 508–516; *Women in the Modern World: Their Education and Their Dilemmas.* Boston: Little, Brown, 1953.

[9] Mead, Margaret. *Male and Female.* New York: W. Morrow, 1949.

[10] Newcomer, Mabel. *A Century of Higher Education for American Women.* New York: Harper Bros., 1959.

[11] Riesman, David. *The Lonely Crowd.* New Haven, Connecticut: Yale University Press; Some Continuities and Discontinuities in the Education of Women. Bennington, Vermont: Third John Dewey Memorial Lecture, 1956.

[12] Sanford, Nevitt. Changing Sex Roles, Socialization, and Education. In Henry, William (Ed.). *Human Development Bulletin,* University of Chicago, Human Development Student Organization, 1958, 58–75.

[13] Sysiharju, Anna-Liisa. *Equality, Home, and Work: A Socio-psychological Study on Finnish Student Women's Attitudes Towards the Woman's Role in Society.* Mikkelissä, Finland: Lansi-Savon Kirjapaino, 1960.

[14] De Beauvoir. *The Second Sex.*

[15] Friedan, Betty. *The Feminine Mystique.* New York: Norton, 1963.

[16] Rudikoff, Sonya. Feminism Reconsidered. *Hudson Review,* 1956, **9,** 178–198.

[17] See Chapters 4 and 7 for a description of the sample.

there ways in which they could do more? What do you consider to be the ideal position of women in our society? Do you foresee any change in the status of women in this country? What constitutes women's role?"

A prominent thesis of *The Feminine Mystique* by Betty Friedan is that American women have been brainwashed into accepting housewifery, motherhood, and conventional feminine behavior as the "be-all and end-all" of women's existence. This observation is not sustained by empirical study of Vassar students.

When asked "What do you criticize in a woman?" 15 of the 49 Vassar seniors who completed all the interviews answered by describing unpleasant characteristics that seem to have no particular sex reference—for example, intolerance, snobbishness, and selfishness. Seven students replied in ways that bear out the contention of *The Feminine Mystique*. They were critical of qualities that do not accord with traditional feminine behavior. They would criticize a woman for "neglecting her children, being overintellectual, too independent, not feminine and warm, or dogmatic about her career." Two students were ready to condemn "either extreme," that is, being immersed in either homemaking or a career to the exclusion of other activities and interests.

A majority of 25 students, however, criticized the very characteristics that supposedly enter into "the feminine mystique." They were disposed to censure "marriage as the only goal in life, reduction of the self to the husband, leaning on being a woman, superficial social life, pettiness and gossip, not having interests outside of the home and family, being too tied to the children," and the like.

Results of objective testing support the findings of the interview studies. Table 8 presents the responses of three classes of Vassar students to items that tap attitudes toward "women's role." A significant majority of seniors reject the item "I dislike women who disregard the usual social or moral conventions." This represents a significant change from the responses of the freshmen. A large majority of both freshmen and seniors answer "false" to "I like the sweet, 'feminine' type of girl as my friend." Slight majorities of freshmen (53 per cent) and seniors (63 per cent) say "true" to

"If I were a housewife and mother, I would also like much outside work or many other activities at the same time."

TABLE 8

RESPONSES OF FRESHMEN AND SENIORS TO TEST ITEMS DRAWN FROM MASCULINITY-FEMININITY SCALES

Item	Freshmen		Seniors	
	%T	%F	%T	%F
I think I would like the work of a dress designer	47	53	45	55
Usually I would prefer to work with women	9	88***	6	93***
I think I would like the work of a garage mechanic	12	88***	11	89***
I like adventure stories better than romantic stories	21	74***	23	75***
I prefer a shower to a bathtub	52	47	40	60*
I think I would like to drive a racing car	26	74***	34	66*
I very much like hunting	21	74***	16	82***
I would like to be a nurse	29	71**	17	83***
I think I would like the work of a librarian	58	42	23	77***
When I work on a committee, I like to take charge of things	54	45	54	45
I want to be an important person in the community	61	38*	41	59
I would enjoy fame (not mere notoriety)	59	40	73	27**
I would like a career	68	28**	69	31**
I dislike women who disregard the usual social or moral conventions	53	46	25	75***
If I were a housewife and mother I would also like much outside work or many other activities at the same time	53	47	63	37*
I would like to be an executive	45	54	56	44
Many girls are catty and petty	80	20***	72	28**
In general I prefer the company of men to women (in sports, intellectual activities, hiking, theater, conversation, etc.)	67	30**	82	18***
I like the sweet "feminine" type of girl as my friend	33	63*	17	83***

Item	Freshmen		Seniors	
	%T	%F	%T	%F
I like sewing	45	55	43	57
Purely social conversation generally bores me	47	53	52	48
I don't expect to have more than two children	19	80***	16	84***
I have always had goals and ambitions that were beyond anything practical or that seemed capable of being realized	35	65*	32	68*
I would enjoy the experience of living and working in a foreign country	93	7***	90	10***
I have several times had a change of heart about my life work	57	37	48	52
I would like to hunt lions in Africa	25	75***	41	59
I would like to be a singer	37	63*	41	59
My family does not like the work I have chosen (or the work I intend to choose for my life work)	3	96***	7	93***
I have never been sorry that I am a girl	61	39*	54	46
I enjoy reading love stories	83	17***	80	20***
I think I would like the work a forest ranger does	31	69**	28	72**
I would like to be a florist	27	73**	27	73**
I like dramatics	80	20***	79	21***
I like collecting flowers or growing house plants	56	44	54	46
I like to cook	73	27**	77	23***
If I were an artist I would like to draw flowers	43	56	43	57
I enjoy children	95	4***	92	8***
There was never a time in my life when I liked to play with dolls	7	93***	16	84***

NOTE: The percentages presented are pooled means of three classes (*N*'s for freshman classes are 398, 404, and 392; *N*'s for senior classes are 274, 258, and 253). Differences between proportions are significant at the levels indicated for at least two of the three classes. Where percentages do not total 100, the differences result from abstentions.

* $p < .05$ ** $p < .01$ *** $p < .001$

Most of the women who were subjects in this research were not inclined to value conventionally feminine characteristics and behavior; if anything, quite the opposite. This is well illustrated by the response to the item "Many girls are catty and petty," to which a sizable majority of students responded "true." Masculine activities and traits are seen as superior to female ones. These results are in line with the findings of Alex Sherriffs and John McKee[18] that both male and female college students rate women lower than men on the possession of desirable traits.

On the other hand, almost every student aspired to marriage. Various studies show that marriage and motherhood are the primary goals of the great majority of young American women.[19] A poll of the entire senior class from which the interview sample was drawn ($N = 274$) indicated that all but two students replied "yes" to the question of whether they wished to marry. One said "no," the other "maybe." And all but one of the students who wished to marry expressed a desire to have children. As Table 8 indicates, however, 68 per cent of the freshmen and 69 per cent of the seniors say, "I would like a career."

Career and Marriage

Since over half the seniors say that they would like careers, and since these young women wish to marry and to have children as well, the question of conflict arises. When the members of the interview sample were asked whether they foresaw conflict in this area, most answered "no," but with some qualifications.

The standard pattern that the women envisioned was working in their fields or professions until children arrived, foregoing this work for some suitable period while the children were young, and then resuming it. Slightly over half of these career-minded young women said that they did not anticipate conflict when the time came to interrupt their careers. "Deep down, marriage is more important," said one of them.

A sizable minority of the career-minded women anticipated

[18] Sherriffs, Alex C., and McKee, John P. Qualitative Aspects of Beliefs about Men and Women. *Journal of Personality,* 1957, **25,** 451–464.

[19] Rosenberg, M. *Occupations and Values.* Glencoe, Illinois: Free Press, 1957.

that interrupting their careers would not be easy, but that it would be necessary. Remarks of this kind characterized these students: "I don't want to devote all my time to my children, but I have to." A quarter of the students did not plan to stop working except for brief periods before and after confinement. One of these young women said, "It may make life miserable for my husband, but I intend to continue my career." Needless to say, the students who wished to work before marriage or before the arrival of children, but who were not committed to careers, anticipated no conflict. Many of them reported that they hoped to remain very much alive intellectually and to retain interests outside the home, but that they would be happy to center their lives on home and family.

When students who reply "true" to "I would like a career" are compared with students who reply "false," a number of significant differences emerge. These comparisons were carried out for the three classes for which responses were presented in Table 8. For each scale, analyses were carried out separately for the freshman and senior test results. Only two scales yield significant differences on the freshman tests. On the Achievement via Independence Scale of the California Psychological Inventory,[20] the "true" respondents score higher at the .001 level of significance,[21] and on the Ethnocentrism Scale,[22] they are lower at the .01 level.

Differences are more numerous on the senior tests. Students who say "true" score higher on the Delinquency Scale of the California Psychological Inventory ($p < .05$), on the Psychasthenia ($p < .01$) and F ($p < .001$) Scales of the Minnesota Multiphasic Personality Inventory,[23] and on the Impulse Expression[24] ($p < .05$), Developmental Status[25] ($p < .001$), and Social Maturity[26] ($p < .05$)

[20] Gough. *Manual for the California Psychological Inventory.*

[21] The difference between proportions reported in this chapter are significant at the levels indicated in at least two of the three classes.

[22] Adorno *et al. The Authoritarian Personality.*

[23] Hathaway and McKinley. *Manual for the Minnesota Multiphasic Personality Inventory.*

[24] Sanford *et al.* Impulse Expression as a Variable of Personality.

[25] Webster. Changes in Attitude During College.

[26] Webster *et al.* A New Instrument for Studying Authoritarianism in Personality.

Scales of the Vassar Attitude Inventory.[27] The "true" respondents are lower on the Social Integration Scale[28] ($p < .05$) of the Vassar Attitude Inventory and on the Authoritarianism ($p < .05$)[29] and Ethnocentrism ($p < .05$) Scales as well.

These test differences suggest that the students who say "true" to "I would like a career" are somewhat more intellectual, unconventional, independent (perhaps rebellious), and flexible in thinking and outlook. They are also somewhat more alienated or isolated socially. It is interesting to observe that these differences are greatly sharpened by college attendance, that is, the differences are most pronounced on the senior tests. Results for the Ethnocentrism Scale, significant on both the freshman and senior tests, are in line with findings of other studies[30] which demonstrate that attitudes toward the role and behavior of women are likely to accord with attitudes toward members of outgroups or "underprivileged" groups. Individuals, including women themselves, who hold somewhat stereotyped views of Negroes or foreigners, for example, are likely to adhere to traditional or rather fixed notions of what is appropriate activity for women.

The Ideal Position of Women in American Society

The above findings suggest that most college women are content with the current status of educated women in the United States, and the interviews bear out this impression. A small group

[27] Webster *et al. Research Manual for VC Attitude Inventory and VC Figure Preference Test.*

[28] A high score on the Social Integration Scale indicates a tendency to go along with the majority in responding to items. The general theme conveyed by a high score is "Pollyannalike," that is, "Everything is fine with me and with the world."

[29] Adorno *et al. The Authoritarian Personality.*

[30] Adelson, Joseph. A Study of Minority Group Authoritarianism. *Journal of Abnormal and Social Psychology,* 1953, **48,** 477–485; Christie, Richard, and Cook, Peggy. A Guide to Published Literature Relating to the Authoritarian Personality Through 1956. *Journal of Psychology,* 1958, **45,** 171–199; Saenger, Gerhart, and Flowerman, Samuel. Stereotypes and Prejudicial Attitudes. *Human Relations,* 1954, **7,** 217–238; Titus, H. Edwin, and Hollander, E. P. The California F Scale in Psychological Research: 1950–1955. *Psychological Bulletin,* 1957, **54,** 47–64.

of students were critical of those women who work outside the home after the birth of children and who compete with men professionally. Another small group felt that reconciliation of their family responsibilities and career aspirations would be a difficult process. But the great majority believed that American society offered them, and educated women generally, ample opportunity for fulfillment. In reply to the question "Do you feel, as a woman, that the future offers too many choices, not enough choices, or sufficient choices?" only four students answered "not enough." (None said "too many.")

In response to the questions "At what period of history and in what area of the world has woman attained her greatest realization?" and "At what period of history and in what area of the world has woman been reduced to her lowest state?" the great majority of students indicated that they considered the current status of women in the United States to be quite all right. This is not to say that they did not recognize certain kinds of professional discrimination against women or attempts to restrain women intellectually. They were aware of these things, but they refused to take them very seriously. The prevailing attitude was that no barriers to women's development are insurmountable, and that a woman can do whatever she wishes, provided she has the appropriate capabilities.

In reply to the question "What do you consider to be the ideal position of women in our society?" seven students emphasized the role of wife and mother almost to the exclusion of other activities; one said, for example, "They should devote themselves to the family and not try to prove that they are the equal of men." Six students stressed rather the opposite position—for example, that a woman should be "anything other than just a *Hausfrau*." The remainder accentuated conditions of equality and freedom for women. "Not to be prevented from doing what she wants" or being "accepted as an equal human being" were typical views of the ideal condition of women.

Most students anticipated even greater independence and equality for women in the future. The interview sample was asked: "Do you foresee any change in the status of women in this country?" The following remarks give the tenor of the replies: "There will be greater emphasis on being a person rather than a woman";

women will be "less of an oddity in business, politics, and the professions." Nine students expressed some disapproval of such trends. "Too bad," said one. "I hate to see women lose their sex." Several of these students wondered, in fact, whether some reversal of the trends toward increasing equality and freedom might set in. "There may be a revolt by men someday," one speculated.

Attitudes toward Feminism

Perhaps what stands out most in studies of attitudes toward the issues of women's role, marriage, and careers is the relaxed quality of the women involved. They are simply not excited about the things that aroused educated women prior to World War II. Many students are quite explicit about this. They regard the emotional fervor of the feminists of the nineteenth and early twentieth centuries as passé and a little bit odd. The feminist ethos somehow belongs with bustles or cloche hats; it is a thing of the past. The sense of membership in an underprivileged group or the feeling of being involved competitively with men in professions or occupations no longer moves women students. They do not perceive society or men as imposing restrictions upon their development or behavior. Margaret Bruton[31] has also noted differences of this sort between the post-World War II generation of young women and their mothers.

Consider the remarks of a very gifted student planning on graduate work and a professional career: "Women will always want marriage and a family first. Feminism is dying out. The older feminists must know they've missed something." Another young woman, also an excellent student with plans for graduate work and a career, said: "Conflict between career and marriage is not necessary. We're not content with subordination, but we've outgrown feminism."

Interviews with Vassar alumnae of the Classes 1929–35[32] in-

[31] Bruton, Margaret P. Present-Day Thinking on the Woman Question. *Annals of the American Academy of Political and Social Science,* 1947, **251,** 10–16.

[32] See Chapters 5 and 6 and Freedman. Studies of College Alumni.

dicate that the decision to embark on a career in those years was often made in the face of clear recognition that such a choice might well preclude marriage. This is not the case today. For example, since World War II, there has been an increasingly higher incidence of marriage among women with advanced degrees.[33]

In keeping with their disposition to be critical of institutions but tolerant and noncensorious of individuals,[34] students tend not to criticize other students who espouse different ways of life. The women who value careers, for example, or intellectual, social, or artistic enterprise, are accepting of those students who regard home and family as all-encompassing. It is this latter group of students, in fact, who possess the strongest feeling about the various issues involved in women's role. Perhaps because of their minority position, there is some tendency among young women in this group to be critical of those women who invest deeply of themselves in activities outside the home and family.

In recent decades, social scientists[35] have emphasized the contradiction and conflict in the lives of educated women. Women who have been educated to value accomplishment are frustrated in the role of housewife. Housewifery is not valued in American society—at least not to the extent that intellectual or professional accomplishment is. On the other hand, for whatever reason, perhaps because of the many roles they must play and the many demands made upon them, educated women are not likely to arrive at the same sense of fulfillment in their work as men.

The majority of graduating seniors hope to pursue a career, and many of these young women anticipate being able to manage both a family and activities outside the home. One wonders at their enthusiastic optimism concerning the future, when their elders are often less sanguine. A. M. Rose[36] has remarked that young women

[33] McBride. Alumnae—Bryn Mawr College.

[34] See Chapter 3.

[35] Jahoda and Havel. Psychological Problems of Women in Different Social Roles; Komarovsky. Cultural Contradictions and Sex Roles; Wallin, Paul. Cultural Contradictions and Sex Roles: A Repeat Study. *American Sociological Review,* 1950, **15,** 288–293.

[36] Rose, Arnold M. The Adequacy of Women's Expectations for Adult Roles. *Social Forces,* 1951, **30,** 69–77.

tend to be more unrealistic than men in planning the future. They are often unaware of contradictions in their expectations. Mirra Komarovsky[37] talks about the light-hearted impracticality that often characterizes the plans of undergraduate women. David Riesman[38] has pointed out that students' attitudes toward economic matters display a similar lack of awareness of the stern facts of daily life. For example, students are likely to describe their future material aspirations as consisting of a ten-room house in the suburbs, several acres of land, two cars, and a summer cabin; then they say, in response to the question of what they expect their annual family income to be, "$10,000."

May we think, then, that in their youthful exuberance and inexperience the students in this study are simply unaware of the harsh realities of the future? Many writers think so. Betty Friedan talks of "the problem that has no name." She says: "It is no longer possible to ignore that voice, to dismiss the desperation of so many American women."[39] The women she is describing are trapped housewives. Simone de Beauvoir describes a housewife: ". . . now she is married, and before her there is no *other* future, this is to be her whole lot on earth. She knows just what her tasks are to be: The same as her mother's. Day after day the same rites will be repeated. As a girl she had nothing, but in dreams she hoped for everything. Now she has her bit of earth, and she thinks in anguish: 'Only this, forever. Forever, this husband, this dwelling.' She has nothing to await, nothing important to wish for."[40] Further, there is abundant testimony by psychotherapists to the prevalence of bored and frustrated housewives.

Undoubtedly, the young women in this research are disposed by their youth and inexperience to overlook certain of the complexities of adult life. But is their vision of the future so wrong? As I have suggested elsewhere, "The rather commonly accepted notion of the specter of Satan stalking our upper-middle-class suburbs in

[37] Komarovsky. Cultural Contradictions and Sex Roles.

[38] Riesman, David. The "Jacob Report." *American Sociological Review,* 1958, **28,** 732–738.

[39] Friedan. *The Feminine Mystique,* p. 26.

[40] De Beauvoir. *The Second Sex,* p. 458.

the form of alcoholism, adultery, loneliness, and feelings of lack of fulfillment of one sort or another [does] not seem at all appropriate."[41] Clearly there are many bored and frustrated middle-aged educated women, but their numbers have been exaggerated by generalizing from the special samples who frequent psychotherapists' offices or who bare their souls to social scientists and journalists.

Reasons for the Revival of the Primacy of Home and Family

The vision of complete equality of the sexes, of no division of labor except for activities directly related to biology—for example, the labor of childbirth—has been abandoned. Betty Friedan places the blame for this on such influences as Sigmund Freud's limited views of women, educators who emphasize sex differences, and advertising men who are interested in capitalizing on housewifery and domesticity for sales purposes. She, like Simone de Beauvoir, rejects or ignores considerations of unconscious determination of behavior. In the view of both these critics, modern educated woman is faced with a rational choice among alternative paths of behavior, and she is choosing the wrong one. To account for behavior as complex as that of educated women in American life, however, one must look to the unformulated or half-formulated, dimly perceived feelings of the individual woman.

As Sonya Rudikoff[42] points out, we must note that masculine and feminine roles cannot be equated with masculine and feminine natures. Roles are observable and manipulable; they are appropriate concepts for social research. But we may not assume that the social personality and the sexual personality are the same. "Anatomy is destiny," said Freud. This is a remark with which most social research has yet to come to grips. This is not to say, of course, that immutable masculine or feminine natures exist or that biology is crucial to consideration of the role of the educated woman in a complex society. Our profound ignorance of this aspect of the problem must be recognized, however.[43]

[41] Freedman. Studies of College Alumni, p. 870.

[42] Rudikoff. Feminism Reconsidered.

[43] Barry, Herbert A., III, Bacon, Margaret, and Child, Irvin L. A Cross-Cultural Survey of Some Sex Differences in Socialization. *Journal of Abnor-*

A prominent theme running through the Vassar interviews is reluctance on the part of young women to threaten the status or security of men by exceptional accomplishment. Careful attention to the qualities which underlie courtship and marriage among college students suggests that in many cases the man's need for security, intimacy, and affection are greater than those of the woman. On the basis of a study of married undergraduate students at Stanford University, David Nyberg[44] wrote: "It appears that college men are more dependent and more anxious than the women they marry—these data suggest that it probably is not accurate to maintain that a girl comes to college 'to hunt a husband.' It is likely to be she who is hunted." In all events, it may well be that an increase in the scope and power of educated women will have to wait upon educated men's recapturing the confidence and competence that they have somehow lost in the contemporary scheme of things.[45]

---

mal and Social Psychology, 1957, **55,** 327–332; Gough, Harrison G. Identifying Psychological Femininity. *Educational and Psychological Measurement,* 1952, **12,** 427–439; Honzik, Marjorie D. Sex Differences in the Occurrence of Materials in the Play Constructions of Preadolescents. *Child Development,* 1951, **22,** 15–35; Pintler, Margaret H., Phillips, Ruth, and Sears, Robert R. Sex Differences in the Projective Doll Play of Preschool Children. *Journal of Psychology,* 1946, **21,** 73–80; Anastasi, Anne. *Differential Psychology.* New York; Macmillan, 1958; and Sherriffs and McKee. Qualitative Aspects of Beliefs About Men and Women, for example, report relationships between personality characteristics and sex which may be discerned rather early in life. The origins of these differences, whether physical (endocrinological or chemical perhaps) or the result of early learning experiences, are obscure.

[44] Nyberg, David. An Immodest Speculation, Supported by Modest Data, Concerning Some Motivations and Circumstances of College Student Marriage. Palo Alto, Calif.: Stanford University, 1965 (Mimeographed).

[45] See Chapter 8.

10

Women and Work

James Boswell reports that Samuel Johnson said: "Sir, a woman's preaching is like a dog's walking on his hinder legs. It is not done well; but you are surprised to find it done at all."[1] This kind of sentiment still prevailed in the latter half of the nineteenth century, when college education for women was first becoming a feature of the American national scene. But by 1920, around the time the franchise was extended to women, notions about their intellectual inferiority had been fairly well dispelled.

In colleges and universities today, except in certain technical and scientific fields which possess a masculine aura, it is taken for granted that women will receive higher grades than men. On tests of verbal aptitude, women score consistently higher. In fields such as English literature, in which there are high concentrations of women, they usually constitute a substantial majority of the honors graduates. Women receive more favorable scores than men on vari-

[1] Boswell, James. *The Life of Samuel Johnson.* Garden City, New York: Doubleday, 1946, p. 169.

ous nonintellective or noncognitive measures of personality characteristics in college students. On tests or scales which reveal a progression between freshman and senior year, freshman women are more like seniors than freshman men are. These differences are not large, but they tend to be consistent.

No one would now argue that women do not possess the requisite qualities of intellect and character to deal with the demands of college education. And no one would now argue that women lack the competence to assume important positions in society—to be doctors, lawyers, business executives, or public officials. Granted that they can do all these things—and do them well—the question is why they are not doing so, at least not in large numbers. Only one-third to two-fifths of American college students are women, and aside from a few fields which attract women, for example, elementary school teaching or social work, the proportion of women in professions or occupations which demand considerable intelligence and education is small. Many educated women are not working outside of the home at all, and the majority of those who are working for remuneration outside the home are engaged in enterprises which do not fully utilize their abilities and knowledge.

The situation is something like the disillusionment with the working class that the Fabian socialists experienced in the early decades of this century. In 1900 the members of the Fabian Society presumed that, given an adequate wage, reasonable working hours, and a fair amount of leisure time, British workers would take to attending public lectures, reading John Stuart Mill, and playing Mozart quartets. Given reasonable working hours, considerable leisure, and at least much improved wages, British workers have taken instead to frequenting dog tracks and Hollywood films and to reading newspapers which report in minute detail scandals and crimes of violence.

Educated women have been a comparable disappointment. Social critics who are in the old feminist tradition, such as Simone de Beauvoir and Betty Friedan, argue that modern educated woman has relinquished the hard-won gains of the feminist movement. For some 50 to 75 years, women struggled to attain equality with men. And when they had attained this equality, or were on the verge of attaining it, they no longer wanted it. Instead of attempting to fulfill themselves in the world of work, they have returned to the primacy of home and family.

Proponents of the rightful place of women as equal or equivalent to that of men are sorely vexed by the defections of modern educated women. Nor are these critics prepared to accept the situation. They continue to exhort college women and alumnae to realize themselves in the world of work or art in the same fashion as men.

In my judgment, many or most of these appeals to educated women are flawed by both inaccurate observation and faulty interpretation of the observations made. We will recall that Betty Friedan talks of "the problem that has no name"—the "desperation" of "trapped" housewives.[2] In a similar vein, I quote from a recent article by two psychologists: ". . . few women are able to make a full and lifetime job from reduced family roles—and to remain satisfied and content in their later years."[3] As Chapter 9 indicates, my observations simply do not accord with this perception of things. Feelings of frustration and a sense of emptiness and lack of accomplishment are not widespread among educated women of middle age.

There has been opposition, and I think rightly so, to certain ramifications of the psychoanalytic concept of penis envy in the development of women. Too often the doctrine of penis envy has been used by adherents of conservative positions vis à vis women to justify their stand. Frequently the motives of women who wish to accomplish something of importance in work or in art are impugned. Such women are called neurotic. If only they had insight into the infantile origins of their competitive strivings with men, the argument goes, they would give up all that nonsense.

While too much importance has been attached, in my view, to some of Sigmund Freud's remarks about a sense of organic inferiority in women, I do not think that sufficient attention has been given to one of his observations: "She gives up her wish for a penis

[2] Friedan. *The Feminine Mystique.*

[3] Keniston, Ellen and Kenneth. The Image of Women and Work. *The American Scholar,* Summer 1964, 369.

and puts in place of it a wish for a child. . . ."[4] As I see it, then, the satisfactions that accrue to most women in bearing and nurturing children provide a tremendous store of contentment. Women who have raised families are likely to feel fulfilled. Other investigators, David Riesman,[5] for example, have observed the relative placidity and complacency of the educated woman in her role as wife and mother, and Alvan Barach[6] has remarked on the failure to consider "love" in discussions of the problems of women in western society.

As Chapter 9 indicates, most college women are not in conflict about working except when it may interfere with rearing children. They do not regard working as unfeminine behavior. There seems to be much confusion about this among social scientists. Ellen and Kenneth Keniston say: ". . . it is a rare working woman in whom inner conflict does *not* complicate the practical problems of combining marriage and career, for whom working is not accompanied by silent questions about her adequacy and by implicit apprehension about her 'envy' of men, and who does not at some level consider a career a denial rather than an expression of femininity."[7] These observations do not seem to be accurate. Interviews with middle-aged alumnae demonstrate that the stock market crash of 1929 and subsequent Depression dispelled the notion that it was somehow improper for a lady to work. Even those women who have not themselves worked have raised their daughters with the expectation that paid work was fitting and proper activity.[8]

Most educated women do not view work as undermining their identity as women. How is it, then, that so many educated women are not working outside the home or are working at jobs which are

[4] Freud, Sigmund. Some Psychological Consequences of the Anatomical Distinction between the Sexes. In Strachey, James (Ed.). *Collected Papers of Sigmund Freud.* London: Hogarth Press and The Institute of Psycho-Analysis, 1950, Vol. 5, p. 195.

[5] Riesman, David. Two Generations. *Daedalus,* Spring 1964, **93,** 711–735.

[6] Barach, Alvan. The Omission of Love in Current Discussions of Women. New York: 1050 Fifth Avenue, 1965 (Mimeographed).

[7] Keniston. The Image of Women and Work.

[8] See Chapter 6 and Freedman. Studies of College Alumni.

beneath their talents? The answer is marriage—which, these days, means early marriage. Marriage and children are the primary goals. The readiness of young women willingly to forego other pursuits or inclinations in the interest of marriage has long been a feature of American life. Alexis de Tocqueville remarked on it: ". . . no American woman falls into the toils of matrimony as into a snare held out to her simplicity and ignorance. She has been taught beforehand what is expected of her, and voluntarily and freely enters upon this engagement. She supports her new condition with courage, because she chose it."[9] Despite boredom with housework, diapers, and the like, marriage and children are satisfying experiences for most women.

When possible, as Edna Rostow points out,[10] educated women are disposed to accommodate interesting work outside the home to family life. The barriers to accomplishing this are considerable, however. Housekeepers and servants are no longer easy to find. It is difficult to interrupt a career for childbirth and then resume it. These days husbands move frequently for business or professional reasons, making it difficult for their wives to put down professional or occupational roots. Given the satisfactions of marriage and motherhood and the difficulties of working outside of the home, the home is likely to win out, particularly in these affluent times in which the income of the wife is not likely to be necessary for living the "good life."

Those critics who feel that women's individual fulfillment or the needs of American society demand greater participation from them in the world of work have proposed certain social changes which would facilitate such work. They suggest, for example, that more part-time positions be offered to women, that arrangements for nursery care be improved, or that communities be physically reconstituted so that long periods of commuting between residential areas and places of work could be eliminated. To my mind, social rearrangements of this kind do not strike at the basic issues.

The heart of the matter is this. After the arrival of children,

[9] De Tocqueville. *Democracy in America,* Vol. 2, p. 246.

[10] Rostow, Edna. Conflict and Accommodation. *Daedalus,* Spring 1964, **93,** 736–760.

most women are not motivated to make the effort to work outside the home unless they need to do so for financial reasons. Why? Part of the explanation has to do with the fact that men feel threatened by women who can or do surpass them professionally or intellectually. Frequently college women scale down their aspirations between freshman and senior year,[11] shifting to professions or activities which are not so prestigious. They do so to some extent because of greater realism, greater awareness of the impediments to achieving their original goals; but also they do so because they sense that men have difficulty in accepting high achievement by women. Until educated men possess more strength and integrity, it will be difficult for many women to set their sights high. Critics of the situation of educated women in American society frequently point to the freedom and opportunity afforded women in other countries, for example, the Scandinavian states or Russia. Yet even in these countries women seldom attain places or positions of preeminence. In all the pictures of the reviewing stand in Red Square on May Day that I have looked at for many a year, women are rare indeed.

It is rather to the issue of the place and meaning of traditional work that we must look for the answer to the question of why more educated women are not working for remuneration outside the home. The basic reason is simply that the vast majority of jobs and professional activities are uninteresting, unrewarding, and lacking in fulfillment. The Romantic poets told the world a long time ago that this was to be one of the consequences of science and the Industrial Revolution. This vision emerged from the mind of Karl Marx as the concept of "alienated work." Educated women wish to do something interesting outside of the home; but that "something interesting" is hard to find.

I do not think that women are likely to accept the contemporary world of work as a measure of accomplishment or fulfillment. Dedicated participation by women will require new roles and new

[11] In a study carried out by Carl Bereiter and Mervin Freedman at Vassar College, changes in level of career aspirations between freshman and senior year were investigated in a sample of 255 students. Twenty-three students had raised their level of career aspiration, 148 indicated no change, and 84 had lowered their aspirations.

ways of work which perhaps only women can provide. I quote from Erik Erikson on this subject.

> An emancipated woman thus does not necessarily accept comparisons with more "active" male proclivities as a measure of her equivalence, even if and after it has become quite clear that she can match man's performance and competence in most spheres of achievement. True equality can only mean the right to be uniquely creative. We may well hope, therefore, that there is something in woman's specific creativity which has waited only for a clarification of her relationship to masculinity (including her own) in order to assume her share of leadership in those fateful human affairs which so far have been left entirely in the hands of gifted and driven men. . . . Mankind now obviously depends on new kinds of social inventions and on institutions which guard and cultivate that which nurses and nourishes, cares and tolerates, includes and preserves.[12]

If humanity is to survive, the sense of integrity and wholeness dissipated with each successive generation since the beginnings of the Industrial Revolution must be restored to the individual personality and to the communities within the larger society. Educated women often have difficulty working outside the home because they grasp intuitively that the work they are being called upon to perform is contributing to the disintegration of the individual personality and to the alienation of people from one another in society. They will dedicate themselves to work outside the home if a way can be found to redefine the world of work in ways that contribute to more humane ends.

In this quest the divorcement of women from the traditional world of work may be an asset rather than an obstruction. Restoration of unity and wholeness to the individual and to society calls for a turning away from the incessant demands for manipulation of things and the conquest of outer space. As Erikson has put it, "The Ultimate . . . may well be found also in the Immediate, which has

[12] Erikson, Erik. Inner and Outer Space; Reflections on Womanhood. *Daedalus,* Spring 1964, **93,** 605–606.

so largely been the domain of woman and of the inward mind."[13] Perhaps educated women can find ways to give to mankind in an age of mechanization and automation the sense of being truly alive that only children and artists now experience—what William Blake so touchingly described in *Auguries of Innocence.*[14]

> To see a World in a Grain of Sand,
> And a Heaven in a Wild Flower,
> Hold infinity in the palm of your hand,
> And Eternity in an Hour.

Arnold Toynbee[15] has described the situation in ancient Sparta. The men, being highly specialized, fit only for warlike pursuits, were unable to adjust to changing times. The welfare of the state came to rest more and more upon the women who possessed the flexibility to run it. Eventually political and economic power in Sparta passed to the women. May we anticipate that, as the Puritan work ethic breaks down in the face of a technology that produces material abundance with little human effort, educated women will assume more and more prominence in the United States?

[13] Erikson. Inner and Outer Space.

[14] Blake, William. Auguries of Innocence. In Sampson (Ed.). *William Blake's Poetical Works,* p. 171.

[15] Toynbee, Arnold. *The Tragedy of Greece.* Oxford: Clarendon, 1921; *A Study of History.* London: Oxford, 1954.

11

The Future of the Women's College

In a study of a number of Vassar College graduates,[1] the women were asked their views about what an "ideal" college would be like. Their replies were quite uniform. An "ideal" college would be very much like their alma mater—with one exception. It would be coeducational. When questioned about their reasons for making the "ideal" college coeducational, these women indicated that they did not feel that they themselves had been handicapped by attending a women's college; rather they considered coeducation to be the predominant future trend, and they were simply accepting the customs of the time.

Recent educational events indicate that this is by no means an isolated sentiment. Almost every poll of college and high school students indicates a large majority in favor of coeducation at the college level, the proportions often running as high as nine to one. And many if not most of our foremost men's and women's colleges have integrated, at least to some degree. This trend is definitely

[1] See Chapter 6 and Freedman. Studies of College Alumni.

continuing. The number of separate men's and women's colleges is declining from a pre-World War II peak, and it is likely that all but a very small share of the colleges founded in the future will be coeducational from inception. Even some Catholic colleges, long regarded as the bastion of separate education, have fallen in with the trend.

This is not to say that women's colleges are suffering from a lack of students. Most of them, particularly those which enjoy considerable prestige, have a high ratio of applications to acceptances. Nevertheless, the continued existence of the separate women's college is questionable. Where physical proximity to men's colleges has made it possible, women's colleges have often taken the opportunity to merge academically, if not administratively. And in those women's colleges not so "fortunate" as to have men's colleges conveniently located close by, there is considerable uncertainty about the future. I was recently asked to talk at one such isolated women's college on the topic "The Future of the Women's College—Is There One?" Of course, in some of our remaining independent women's colleges, strong voices are still raised in opposition to the coeducational trend, but I have the impression that these voices are growing fainter.

A good question at this point is whether anything really worthwhile would be lost were women's colleges gradually to disappear, or at least to lose their distinct identities. More specifically, since we are considering women's education in particular, could it be that women actually receive a better education in a coeducational college?

There is little to suggest that the women's college possesses any special educational virtue. Except for somewhat greater emphasis on fields in which women are more likely to major, such as performing arts, and the frequent absence of traditionally masculine subjects, such as engineering, there is little difference between the curriculum of the women's liberal arts college and that of a comparable men's or coeducational institution. One liberal arts college seems much like another in this respect. Often we are told that the chief advantages of a separate women's college are the relative absence of dates and social distractions—at least during the week—

and the opportunity to engage in extracurricular activities, for example, clubs or newspaper work, without domination by men. I hardly consider these to be cogent arguments, since I believe that those students who are sufficiently motivated to pursue their studies with energy and enthusiasm at a women's college would behave in the same way at a coeducational school; further, I consider the character and hence the value of extracurricular activities to be very much determined by other more basic qualities of the institution, such as the degree to which independence of spirit and thought is encouraged.

The first women's colleges were founded about 100 years ago with a very active sense of mission. At that time most colleges did not admit women. Indeed the resistance to affording women the same educational opportunities as men was great. So the women's colleges were out to demonstrate that anything men could do educationally could be done equally well by women. For some time, women's colleges were in the forefront of educational innovation in other ways as well. For example, incorporation of creative arts into the liberal arts curriculum and study abroad were contributions of the women's colleges. Graduates of women's colleges were often social innovators, particularly in the nineteenth century, serving in the forefront of the crusade for women's rights and other social reform movements. But with the demise of feminism and of social programs that seem to be of particular concern for women, the sense of mission that characterized the women's colleges in their early days waned. If most women's colleges are now relatively indistinguishable academically from coeducational colleges, why be concerned by the possibility of their disappearing—particularly when there may well be definite advantages for women in being educated with men? Educators generally agree that college men display greater questioning of authority and greater intellectual aggressiveness than women, and that class discussions with men participating are likely to be livelier than those involving only women.

In short, are women's colleges social and educational anachronisms, or can we advance arguments to justify their continued existence? My reply is that we can—most emphatically. First, I would dislike seeing any further departure from the pluralistic quality of the American college structure. Our educational scheme almost defies categorization and description. There are public and private colleges; state, county, and municipal; men's, women's, and coeducational; Catholic, Protestant, and Jewish; and liberal, technical, and all combinations thereof—with a great range of academic and intellectual characteristics within each of these groupings besides. I believe that there is much to be gained from such variety among our colleges. Just as American society has benefited from a multitude of styles and ways of life, so I think our system of higher education may benefit from a number of different kinds of institutions.

More particularly, I believe that there are many important and unique contributions that women's colleges can make to education and to American life. What is needed more than anything else is a return of the missionary zeal that once characterized women's colleges. They should stand for something, as once they did; therein lies the justification of their continued existence. Why must the women's colleges pattern themselves upon the men's colleges? It is hard to improve upon the remarks of Diana Trilling that, as long as women feel inferior to men, they need to get an equally bad education so that they will not feel they have been discriminated against. Women's colleges ought to take the offensive instead of trying to copy the "real thing," the prestigious men's colleges; they should strike higher notes on the educational scale; they should aim at providing some of the educational inspiration and innovation that are so badly needed.

For example, the women's colleges are in a better position than men's colleges to resist some of the antiliberal and antihumanistic pressures in American society. The world is all too much with men's education and men's colleges. As Harold Taylor[2] has pointed out, the American man has fewer educational alternatives because of his automatic commitment to the idea of success. Although prominent educators caution our students and colleges not to overlook humanistic considerations in preparing for business, professional, or

[2] Taylor, Harold. Are Women's Colleges Obsolete? *The New York Times Magazine,* September 7, 1958.

scientific careers, the liberal tradition may all too often receive short shrift in an era of competition and rivalry. We need the women's colleges to restore our aesthetic sense, our awareness of the variousness and complexity of nature and of life. They can remind us of Blake's words: "The tree which moves some to tears of joy is in the Eyes of others only a Green thing that stands in the way."[3]

The women's colleges may serve as bulwarks of academic freedom in times of threat to our traditional liberties. Only a decade ago, fairly strong restrictive pressures were brought to bear on our colleges and universities. This could well happen again, inasmuch as institutions of higher learning are a potent source of opposition to military involvement in Vietnam. By virtue of the private status of most women's colleges, and because they depend to only a slight degree on public support, for example, on government research funds, they can more effectively resist political pressures.

We need not go so far into the needs and problems of society at large, however, to find distinctive roles for our women's colleges. There are still many unresolved issues in women's education and in the lives of educated women that cry out for attention. For one thing, the proportion of college students who are women has decreased considerably in recent decades. In 1930, there were about as many women as men in our colleges. Now the ratio is something like one to two or two to three.

Or consider, for example, the phenomenon of early marriage among young people. The average age of marriage in the United States is the lowest of any industrialized nation. Many colleges actively support early marriage or at least bow to what seems to be the inevitable by providing housing and other facilities for married students. The public image of these student marriages is highly idealized: the happy young couple sharing their studies and the intellectual life of the campus, freed from the tensions and superficial social life of the unmarried state. The reality is far different in most cases, however. As Kate Hevner Mueller has indicated, in all but a

[3] Blake, William. In Keynes, Geoffrey (Ed.). *The Complete Writings of William Blake*. London: The Nonesuch Press, 1957, p. 793.

small minority of campus marriages, it is only the husband who is the student; the wives are "working their husband's way through college."[4]

In former eras those individuals who did not marry at about the same time as most of their contemporaries were merely regarded as a bit odd. Now, as David Riesman has pointed out, the failure to marry young has taken on almost the quality of something monstrous or unnatural.[5] Too often a commitment to marriage is made before an individual is ready for it, before he has found himself. In such cases, marriage often blocks pathways to higher development. Women's colleges can set themselves the goal of countering the tyranny of early marriage; indeed, in the last few years, several officials of women's colleges have made pronouncements of this kind. But the goal cannot be accomplished simply by issuing statements. Students can be induced to forego the customary social and sexual pleasures of their contemporaries only to the extent that other activities, their studies, for example, have captured their spirit and imagination.[6]

A recent educational innovation which has received much attention is programs which provide special educational opportunities for women who already have considerable schooling, bachelor's degrees, for example. These programs call attention to a gap in the education of women, a need not now filled by much of undergraduate education. Examination of the curriculum in our women's colleges from the point of view of the special problems of women's education may well suggest other reforms or innovations.

Mabel Newcomer has recommended that greater weight be given to professional education in women's colleges.[7] She is disturbed by the increasing number of women who work at jobs below their talents and abilities as the proportion of women at work out-

[4] Mueller, Kate Hevner. The Scope of the Pressures and Opportunities That Face the Educated Woman. Bloomington, Indiana: School of Education, University of Indiana, 1957 (Mimeographed).

[5] Riesman. Two Generations.

[6] See Katz and Sanford. The Curriculum in the Perspective of the Theory of Personality Development.

[7] Newcomer. *A Century of Higher Education for American Women.*

side the home increases. This notion appeals to me for another reason as well. I believe that the traditional liberal arts undergraduate curriculum has done the educated woman a disservice. It has tended to make her a passive appreciator of the work of others, and it has thereby contributed to a sense of inferiority in women. This is one of the reasons why women who are capable of activities of a high order are content to work in subordinate roles and leave the direction of things to men who are frequently their cultural and intellectual inferiors.

As society changes, as our lives change, the unique contributions of the women's college will vary; but the women's college will never outlive its usefulness if it can recapture the spirit and sense of importance it once had. Too often, in the past, the suggestion that there was something special about women's education or a women's college was met with hostility by women scholars. Anyone who was interested in sex differences in education was ipso facto in favor of retaining them—at the expense of women's development, of course.

After more than a decade of study of higher education, I am convinced that women's colleges are special places, in the sense that a higher order of education can go on in them. I believe that they possess the potential for much greater service to society and to their own students than they have performed in recent decades. What is needed in these colleges is imaginative leadership, faculty and administrators who are not apologetic because their college does not have Nobel prize winners on the faculty or because it is located 100 miles from the nearest college with eligible men, but who instead have their gaze fixed on the important issues, female and human, of our nation and of our time.

V

CURRENT ISSUES ON THE CAMPUS

12

Turned On and Tuned Out: Drugs on Campus

Within the last five years, drug use has increased on the American campus. Before that, drugs were used almost exclusively by those clearly out of step with conventional American life. Also, prior to about 1960, taking drugs usually implied physiological addiction, heroin being the substance most used. An exception was marijuana. Certain groups in big cities like Los Angeles and New York, many of them composed of musicians, actors, and writers, smoked "pot" without deleterious physiological effects or interference with their professional activities. Marijuana, however, was very rarely found on college campuses.

Physiologically addictive drugs are still seldom used by college students, but there are now few colleges and universities where marijuana and the new psychedelic drugs, chiefly LSD, are not consumed. On even the most provincial of campuses, a student who has "flipped out" as a result of taking LSD is likely to turn up at the counseling center, or a few students may be expelled for smoking pot in a dormitory. This is not to say that the proportion of students who take drugs is high. Most college students are conventional and dutiful, and are unlikely to contravene accepted standards of behavior in so serious a way. But on campuses where cosmopolitan students congregate—large city campuses or those of prestigious small liberal arts colleges—the proportion of students who experiment with pot or LSD may run as high as 10 or 15 per cent.[1] This is not a large percentage, but the total numbers are considerable. In a student body of 15,000, for example, only 2 per cent equals 300 students—a figure not easily ignored. And the number of drug users seems to be growing.

It is difficult to build a serious case against smoking marijuana, except that a user will find himself in serious trouble if he is caught by the police.[2] The effects on society at large, were smoking pot to become as ubiquitous as the consumption of alcohol, are unknown; but within the current limits of use, there is little evidence that marijuana directly damages the individuals who smoke it.[3] Occasionally a person of somewhat precarious emotional stability may be thrown into a panic state or even a psychosis as a result of smoking pot, but this seldom happens.[4] Similarly, there is little basis for asserting that smoking pot is often a prelude to self-destructive

[1] The proportion of pot smokers exceeds 10 per cent on only a few campuses. Users of marijuana outnumber ingestors of LSD. Some sort of folk wisdom seems to be at work among students. They recognize that they may experiment with marijuana without the likelihood of harm (except for arrest by police), whereas LSD presents greater psychological hazards. Among students, a high proportion of LSD ingestors smoke pot. Smaller proportions of pot smokers take LSD, however. Among students, in short, marijuana does not lead inevitably to more potent or dangerous drugs.

[2] In California, for example, possession of marijuana is a felony, a serious offense indeed.

[3] As with alcohol, one has to learn how to handle marijuana "wisely." Howard Becker has described how it is that one learns the "marijuana experience." Becker, Howard. *Outsiders: Studies in the Sociology of Deviance.* Glencoe, Illinois: Free Press, 1963.

[4] Goodman, Louis, and Gilman, Alfred. Cannabis. In *The Pharmacological Basis of Therapeutics.* New York: Macmillan, 1965, pp. 299–301; Sollman, Torald. *A Manual of Pharmacology.* Philadelphia: Saunders, 1957, p. 314; Williams, I. G., Himmelsbach, C. K., Wikler, A., Ruble, O. C., and Lloyd, B. J. Studies on Marijuana and Pyrahexyl Compound. *U. S. Public Health Reports,* 1946, **61,** 1059–1083. Research on marijuana is handicapped by lack of a standard product. There are many marijuanas. Research findings based on one type of cannabis may not hold for other kinds.

or socially damaging acts. No data exist, for example, to demonstrate that marijuana contributes significantly to an individual's criminal tendencies.[5] However, a real problem is that once a student steps over the line prohibiting drug use and finds that nothing terrible has happened, it is easy for him to fall into the illusion that there are no dangers at all.

Perhaps the most serious charge that may be made against pot is that it is indirectly psychologically damaging. Since it is officially banned, its use reinforces rebellious and antisocial tendencies. Individuals who smoke pot regularly—as opposed to those who experiment with it on one or a few occasions—are likely to scoff at such a remark. Divorced as they are from traditional American culture and society, they are hardly frightened by the prospect of further alienation. Indeed, they are apt to welcome it.

The consistent pot smokers are usually graduate students in the arts, philosophy, the humanities, and to some extent, the social sciences. The rebellion they express in many ways, including smoking pot, stems from their disillusionment with American life and values. They oppose American intervention in Vietnam; they are angered by the lot of Negroes and other disadvantaged minority groups. And they are often militant. Aside from enjoying pot's intrinsic satisfactions—relaxation and heightened sensibility, for example—these students get pleasure from sharing a rebellious, illegal activity.[6] The more rebellious or "anti" the movement, the greater the likelihood that pot smokers will be drawn to it. In contrast, the use of marijuana is rare among Peace Corps and antipoverty volunteers. Even though these workers may oppose traditional policies and politics, their activities are more a gesture of social affirmation than of protest.

[5] Statements concerning relationships between smoking pot and illegal activity seem to be based on populations in which crime rates are fairly high —lower-class urban Negroes, for example. As use of marijuana becomes something of a middle-class phenomenon, it is likely that the correlation between smoking pot and other illegal activities will be lower.

[6] It may be that many young people need to engage in some activity which does not have the approval of conventional society. In this sense smoking pot has the rakish quality that accompanied drinking before alcohol attained wide acceptance in American life.

On any cosmopolitan campus today or in any large city, a student can easily buy marijuana or a psychedelic drug. About 80 psychedelic or consciousness-expanding substances have been identified in the western world—morning glory seeds, peyote, and psilocybin are among the more prominent—but LSD, the most powerful, has preempted the field. Because of its shadowy legal status, it has often been easier to obtain than the clearly illegal marijuana. Revisions of federal drug laws have altered the status of LSD,[7] but at least in the near future there is little likelihood that pot or LSD will be in short supply. Connections, sometimes students, often ex-students, are easy to find. The going rate is five dollars for an LSD capsule.[8]

Although the users of marijuana and LSD overlap, these drugs have assumed quite different meanings for the students who ingest them. Smoking pot is likely to be a relaxing, convivial affair. One may occasionally undergo profound mystical or self-revelatory experiences while smoking marijuana, but few pot enthusiasts would claim that it initiates one into life's deepest mysteries. Devotees of LSD, on the other hand, have surrounded the ingestion of this substance with a mystique, with cults, with rituals. Some students claim that LSD experiences provide deep insights. They say they have seen themselves with a clear eye, stripped of the defenses and artifices which ordinarily hedge perception. A better self, an ideal self, may be envisioned. New powers are made available to them; intense mystical or religious experiences occur.

However, not all ingestions of LSD result in revelatory trips. Sometimes nothing happens. Other times, the reaction may be limited to minor perceptual distortion. The setting in which LSD is taken considerably influences the effect. For some students, an LSD trip is a profound personal experience; for others it becomes a religion, a way of life. These two kinds of LSD enthusiasm—the profound personal experience versus the way of life—tend to divide on the frequency of dosage. Students for whom LSD has not become a way of life probably have experienced only a few LSD trips—

[7] Recent federal action limits the manufacture and distribution of LSD. Several states, in addition, have added LSD to the roster of illegal drugs.

[8] Recent restrictive legislation has resulted in higher prices.

three or four perhaps, spaced at intervals of several months. LSD experience is likely to contribute to their alienation and to spur them on to rebel all the more vehemently against conventional American life and politics.

When LSD becomes a religion or a way of life, however, students take it more frequently—once a week perhaps, or even more often. And when this occurs, a student is likely to leave school. A number of large universities now have groups or cults of LSD devotees who live in the vicinity. Most of the members are ex-students. These people are turned on to their inner world, their internal experience. The external world is tuned out. They do little except observe. They are great nature lovers. They will journey to places of unusual natural beauty, turn on with LSD, and look. They work spasmodically, when funds are needed, but otherwise they are inactive. The preoccupations of most people—educational, professional, political—are "games" to them. There is the "Vietnam-Administration game," the "student-college administration game," the "Hitler-Jewish game," the "McCarthy-ADA game," and the like. Their living conditions often become squalid. They are in tune with infinity, and anyone who is involved with the activities of the external world is dismissed as being unenlightened.

Communication between the LSD users and the unenlightened is limited. Because so much of what occurs during an LSD trip is nonverbal, little can be reported. LSD enthusiasts talk of religious conversions, the awakening of artistic creativity, the reconciliation of opposites. The main change to be observed in such individuals, however, is that they have given up doing anything. The aspiring painter talks of the heightening of his aesthetic sensibilities, but he has stopped painting. The graduate student in philosophy talks of the wondrous philosophical theories he has evolved, but he has stopped writing his dissertation. It seems that the world of fantasy has become far more compelling than the world of involvement with external things. Indeed, fantasy is substituted for reality. If one has dreamed the plot of a great novel, the work of actually writing it is too much trouble.

Much has been made of the psychological perils of LSD. They are real enough. In San Francisco, Los Angeles, or New York, one could doubtless track down several hundred cases of people who have become psychotic as a result of a dose of LSD.[9] Each student health service, psychiatric clinic, or emergency service of a general hospital would yield a number of such cases. Most of these episodes are of short duration. For each instance of an individual's "flipping out," there are several of panic reaction to an LSD experience. Tranquilizers will terminate the physiological effects of LSD in such instances. Most of these reactions occur when LSD is taken in unfavorable settings—alone in a room, or in uncongenial company. The impairment of judgment that may accompany an LSD trip is probably more serious. It is often difficult to determine the duration of the experience. Individuals whose customary judgment is still somewhat impaired may be driving cars, teaching classes, or making decisions about important family matters.

The long-range physiological results of such a powerful stress reaction as an LSD experience are unknown. Some authorities believe that repeated ingestions of LSD may have enduring or permanent adverse effects. The semidazed quality displayed by some individuals who are on LSD a good part of the time may be at least partially physiological in origin. It is unlikely that one or only a few ingestions of LSD will have enduring physiological effects, but definitive data are not yet at hand.

It is in quietism that the chief danger of LSD lies. An affluent and complex society can easily afford small groups of people whose chief commitment is to their internal processes and their fantasy worlds. But what if there were many such? It is ironic that the military establishments of both Russia and the United States, the very groups that epitomize all that the devotees of consciousness expansion most oppose, are reportedly experimenting with LSD as a weapon. A population that is turned on will make no trouble. It will be easy prey for the conqueror. LSD zealots, unlike Mahatma

[9] From September 1965 to April 1966, the incidence of cases of adverse reactions to LSD ranged from five to fifteen per month in the psychiatric emergency service of the Neuropsychiatric Institute of the University of California, Los Angeles, Medical Center. Ungerleider, J. Thomas, Fisher, Duke D., and Fuller, Marielle. The Dangers of LSD. *Journal of the American Medical Association,* 1966, **197,** 109–112.

Gandhi or William Blake, mystics who were committed to the human social struggle, ignore the realities of power.

LSD is unquestionably of potential value in various forms of psychotherapy. It may be used to shatter the habitual modes of reaction of people with strong fixations—alcoholics, recidivist criminals, and compulsives, for example—so that they may evolve new ways of coping with the world and of living with themselves. And undoubtedly psychedelic experiences have entailed for some people profound personal insights and mystical and spiritual experiences. These powers are to be taken seriously.

It is more difficult to take LSD seriously as a religion or a way of life. The notion that in three to six hours one may painlessly attain the wisdom that the Buddha achieved only over a period of years seems ludicrous. The LSD grab bag of philosophy, compounded out of Zen, Erich Fromm, existentialism, Aldous Huxley, and Carl Jung, among others, is an unlikely guide to life in a complex society. The description of a person as "loving" (the ultimate compliment), as if somehow one could touch this entity of love, is right out of adolescent fantasy. Above all, the absence of a tragic sense makes LSD as a religion or way of life no more applicable to the richness of human experience than any other simplistic religion.

Yet the phenomenon of psychedelic experience as a way of life should not be ignored. Why is this life attractive to hundreds of bright and sensitive young people? Why are many thousands of other youths eager to undergo the psychedelic experience? The answers are, of course, many and varied. Transcendentalism and the search for utopia are hardly new to American life. There is, however, an urgency to this quest for new values that deserves the most serious regard.

Many college students are examining the values of the western world and finding them wanting. There is an upsurge of interest in introspection and in the life of the emotions. There is great concern with people rather than with things. Questions of ethics and morality are on their minds as perhaps never before in American life—not since the Civil War, at any rate. And their education is not meeting these interests. The things that are most important to many young Americans are not being discussed in academic life.

The sterile formalism of much American higher education can hardly hold a candle to the psychedelic experience.

The interest of many students in drug experience cannot be dismissed simply as a sign of delinquency, rebelliousness, or psychological pathology. It represents a search for a new way of life. It indicates needs and desires that American society and education do not now meet or fill. There is a quality of naïveté in this quest by students. Wholeness, joy, wisdom, and love are not likely to result from a few hours spent under the influence of a chemical. The interest in drug experience informs us, however, that American society and education are doing little to contribute to the richness of life that students sense can be theirs.

13

Roots of Student Discontent

A pervasive sense of dissatisfaction with American society lies at the root of student discontent, protest, and rebellion. The heart of the matter is that students are being educated to fit into a society they reject, at least in considerable part. This pervasive mood of dissatisfaction must be recognized if the sources of unrest on the various campuses are to be understood. Explanations based on local issues alone—large classes at Michigan, rules governing the use of alcohol at Trinity College in Hartford, women's social regulations and judicial procedures at Stanford, restrictions on freedom of speech and assembly at Berkeley—are incomplete. Similarly, explanations based on traditional politics do not really apply. The social scientists or philosophers who discussed the Free Speech Movement at Berkeley in terms of political disputes and allegiances, after the fashion of the Trotsky-Stalin conflict of the 1930's, were maundering. Connections between political parties or political figures and the leaders of the Free Speech Movement were remote and tenuous.

The hopes, dreams, and desires of college students must be interpreted to their parents, their teachers, and the American public if disasters like the turmoil at Berkeley are not to be repeated. I have talked to students at Berkeley who have learned to their dismay that their parents and their parents' friends still explain the difficulties on that campus as simply the work of radical agitators or beatniks. Likewise, college administrators and faculty members have hardly begun to appreciate the temper of student feeling these days. Of course, many faculty members and administrators concentrate on matters not directly involved with undergraduate students —research and publications, for example, or the expansion of graduate programs. But even when they do turn their attention to the undergraduate, their descriptions and explanations are almost invariably wide of the mark.

To some extent, the feelings and behavior of students must also be interpreted to the students themselves. Many students are unconscious of, or only dimly perceive, the springs of their restlessness and rebellion. This is why minor issues may become the focus of major conflict, and why students often fall prey to leadership that does not serve them well. Inchoate dissatisfaction may be channeled into irrelevant outbursts. The analogy to psychoanalysis and psychotherapy is apposite here: The better students understand themselves, the freer they are to choose among alternative actions, and the more likely they are to choose suitable ones.

Why are our students dissatisfied with so much of American society? Why are they reluctant to fit in? The answer is simple. The Industrial Revolution is ending in the United States. A new era—that of automation and cybernation—is upon us. And the consequences, for the individual and for society, are enormous. Students are restless and dissatisfied because they recognize, or sense, that the education they are receiving is not functional for the world they will be inhabiting in ten or twenty years. Current educational practices and procedures are modeled on the images of men and of work bequeathed to us by the nineteenth century.

I cannot anticipate all the consequences of automation and cybernation. I can, however, discern that students are preparing for a different human and social condition. I quote J. Bronowski, the scientific and moral philosopher:

> The key to the action of living things then is this, that it is directed toward that future. They have a way of knowing what is going to happen next. Most of this knowledge is unconscious. We need not be astonished about this foresight, or at any rate we need not find it more astonishing than we find the rest of the world. For plainly it has always been the condition for the survival of living things, individually and in species. Unless they could adapt themselves to the future, and interpret its signals in advance, they were bound to perish.[1]

Faculty members and college administrators also respond to these evolutionary pressures, but because they are older, the forces of conservatism are stronger within them. Youth is more responsive. Much unrest and conflict on college campuses may be explained as the attempt by students to bend educational procedures to their own requirements and to influence faculty members and administrators for new personal and social ends. These goals are fourfold: (1) the restoration of viable communities in colleges and universities and in society at large; (2) the introduction of unity into the intellect and the personality; (3) the establishment of the ethic of social service as a powerful motive in modern life; (4) the freeing of the impulse life of man—the release of what Henry Murray calls "the erotic imagination."

Rebelliousness and demands for more autonomy are by no means all that is involved in student movements. Students also desire more affiliation with the faculty. They are demanding of administrators, and particularly of teachers, that they join with them to establish that "community of scholars" one hears so much about and so seldom sees.

Given the intense competition of contemporary academic life, a student rarely has the opportunity to cooperate with other people in a venture which has meaning for all the participants. Team sports are lightly regarded by guardians of academic integrity, but such activities provide the student with one of his few opportunities to work with others toward a common end. Ideology aside, teach-

[1] Bronowski. *The Common Sense of Science,* p. 106.

ins appeal to students because they are a chance to work cooperatively with faculty in an enterprise that cuts across traditional teacher-student relationships and activities. Students are attempting to counter the atmosphere of competitiveness and isolation which has prevailed on most campuses for the last two decades. This motive, of which they are often only vaguely aware, accounts for much behavior that on the surface appears to be simple rebellion.

The need for "adult" leadership, faculty leadership in particular, must not be overlooked. Much has been made of the statement, "You can't trust anyone over thirty," which reputedly was one of the slogans of the Free Speech Movement. Yet the leaders of that movement wished to dedicate the steps of Sproul Hall on the Berkeley campus to the late Alexander Meiklejohn, the great civil libertarian, who was over ninety when he died in December 1964. At Berkeley, where the faculty in recent months has become actively involved in issues of the university community, potentially explosive issues have been, or are being, resolved with a minimum of public discord.

The Industrial Revolution diversified labor and knowledge. As the United States was rapidly industrialized in the decades after the Civil War, colleges became increasingly fragmented. Major fields of specialization, departments, and divisions replaced a uniform curriculum and courses which emphasized the synthesis of subject matter. This tendency reached its height in the post-Sputnik era, when young people were urged to specialize in secondary school, or even earlier, so that they might get into the right undergraduate college, which would prepare them for the right graduate or professional school, which in turn would ensure them entrée to important professional or business positions.

College students are becoming increasingly dissatisfied with this process of atomization. They seek breadth and unity in their studies. At many colleges in the last few years, the number of undergraduates who major in broadly defined fields—for example, literature, philosophy, and history—has been increasing at a considerable rate. In an account of National Merit Scholars, Robert Nichols writes: ". . . the interest of able students in physical sciences and engineering has been decreasing . . . [and] interest in the social sciences has been correspondingly increasing."[2] To be sure, such students are women more often than not. But the trend holds for men as well. Although Stanford is very strong in engineering and sciences, the department today with the largest number of undergraduate majors is history, and at Stanford men outnumber women by about two to one. Whitehead's "expert knowledge in some special direction" will not soon disappear at the undergraduate level, but I do believe that by majoring in broadly defined fields, students are attempting to introduce a measure of unity or wholeness into their education.

Activities such as the Peace Corps and the civil rights movement demonstrate that an ethic of social service has recently assumed greater importance in the lives of college students. This ethic of social service reflects their need to be part of communities that have meaning for them; but it is also a response to automation and the economy of affluence. If little human energy is required to sustain human life in excellent material circumstances, a philosophy of life dominated by the aphorisms of Benjamin Franklin becomes dubious. The Puritan or Calvinist ethic of hard work and success in competitive struggle is on the wane. It is becoming increasingly difficult to motivate students to respond to the traditional rewards of western industrial society.

The freeing of the impulse life, or the freeing of Eros in western civilization, has been taking place since the end of World War I. By Eros, I do not mean sexual expression in its physical manifestations only, and I surely do not mean sexual promiscuity.[3] College students are increasingly unwilling to accept education as a grim, humorless, competitive affair. They want more zest, more spirit, more life than has characterized most colleges and universities in recent years. They want to mean it when they sing "Gaudeamus Igitur."

The consequences of these desires and needs of students will be enormous. No facet of personal or social life in the United States will be unaffected. In higher education, the grading system and

[2] Nichols, Robert. Career Decisions of Very Able Students. *Science,* 1964, **144,** 1316.

[3] See Chapters 7 and 8.

comparable procedures for judging students will be drastically altered. A movement to liberalize grading programs is already under way in some American colleges.[4] Antioch, for example, will dispense with grades in the freshman year, and Princeton and Stanford have made it possible for students to receive pass or fail marks rather than letter grades outside their major fields. Princeton students may now "experiment" with courses and disciplines without fear of penalty by way of a lowered grade point average.

Similarly, students will not be dropped for reason of academic failure—at least, not in the first years of college. The system that will emerge is likely to resemble arrangements at Oxford and Cambridge. After some period of time, students will be required to demonstrate an appropriate degree of competence or mastery, but acceptance of the student by a college will mean a commitment to educate him. This commitment dictates retaining him within the institution, except when it may seem that his education would be better served by his leaving. In rare cases, when the presence of a student appears to threaten the welfare of a college, it may be necessary to expel him; but the present system in most colleges and universities, which really places students on trial and demands that they measure up to certain standards under pain of dismissal, will disappear.

Current academic procedures, and teaching and learning situations, will be drastically altered. Much of the burden of conveying routine information—events of history, vocabulary and grammar of foreign languages, basic chemical and mathematical formulas, and so on—will be assumed by programmed instruction. The development of new ways of looking at things will receive increasing attention. To such ends, small groups of faculty members, graduate students, and undergraduates will work together. Age and status variations in such groups will be of minimal importance, since the task of developing new knowledge, new concepts, and new ways of thought will promote humility and a cooperative spirit among the

[4] For a detailed account of recent changes in grading procedures, see Miller, Stuart. Report and Recommendations on Student Evaluation at the University of California, Berkeley. Berkeley, Calif.: University of California, 1965 (Mimeographed).

participants. Since autumn 1965, a large number of seminars have been available to Stanford freshmen.[5] They have been taught by all levels of faculty, from teaching assistants to full professors. Each seminar contains about six freshmen (occasionally fewer in the case of physical sciences) and in some instances an upper division undergraduate. The emphasis in these freshman seminars is on subject matter and activities that tend to be outside traditional curricula and courses. A few illustrative course titles: "Problems Facing the Contemporary Composer," "Authority in Organizations," "The University as a Social Institution."

Traditional divisions into departments and fields of study will assume less and less importance in higher education as time goes by. Many students will have no major subjects of concentration. The assumption that there is a finite body of information which each student in a field of study must absorb will go by the board—to some extent because of concern with new ways of thought and with interdisciplinary programs, but also because the expansion of knowledge will render such universal expertise almost impossible. Curricula suitable to the needs and desires of youth and the world of the future are still in their infancy; but it is certain that traditional major fields of study and courses of specialization are on their way out.

Consider the interest in creativity among educators and social scientists in recent years. As Bronowski has pointed out, the creation of unity out of variety is the same in science as in art.[6] The creative act is the leap of imagination that provides a wholeness which did not previously exist. Newton's remarkable conjunction of apple and moon is of the same order as Keats's association of beauty and truth. No one concerned with devising a curriculum that will foster creativity is likely to confine his attention to the traditional departments and fields of specialization. The same is true of attempts to promote development of such qualities as independence of judgment, logical thinking, or proficiency in communication.

Counseling activities in the high schools and occupational

[5] These seminars are known as the Land Seminars.

[6] Bronowski. *Science and Human Values,* p. 35.

guidance in the colleges will undergo extensive modification. Such counseling is now mainly designed to make it possible for students to fit into one system or another as smoothly as possible. A high school student is aided in choosing the college at which he is likely to be successful—that is, one from which he is likely to graduate with good grades. A college student is helped to choose an occupation or profession for which he has the requisite aptitudes and for which he seems to possess the appropriate interests—interests that resemble those of people who have been successful in the field. The emphasis on development of new knowledge and the reduction of emphasis on grading and failure will change these patterns. Students will be encouraged to try new things—to go to a college, for example, where they will find colleagues of quite different values or personality; or to take courses which may interest them, even if they seem to have little aptitude or ability for them. Counselors, in short, will advise with an eye to the fullest development of individual personality rather than to the perpetuation of traditional professions and occupations.[7]

The concept of self-development as a major goal of life will be a tremendous spur to liberal education in the classic sense. An affluent society in which the labor of young people is not needed will allow students more time before committing themselves to a profession or comparable activity.[8] Young adults will come to resemble the young men of the upper classes in the nineteenth century, who were not expected to do much before they were thirty, except travel and meditate. An eminent foundation recently undertook support of a program whereby a number of students at a prominent men's college will interrupt their education for a year to live and observe —without any specified program or duties—in certain underdeveloped countries.

Some courses of study and corollary professions or occupations —the teaching profession, for one—will benefit from the kinds of trends I have described. Others, such as business, industry, medi-

[7] Mathewson, Robert. Manpower or Persons. *The Personnel and Guidance Journal,* 1964, **43**, 338–342.

[8] At the present time, the draft prohibits such a course of development in young men.

cine, and law, will suffer. The decline of material reward as a motive for entering an occupation or profession and the interest in synthesis of knowledge and interdisciplinary study rather than in specialization will militate against students' adopting such careers. This will be particularly true of the brighter and livelier students. One hopes that major redefinition of these professions and activities will result; and by "major redefinition," I do not mean superficial alterations of public "image" designed to attract good students.

Some professions are already showing signs of change. Law schools have traditionally attracted the more conservative and conventional students. The following news item is from *The Daily Californian,* May 20, 1965: "Ten Boalt Hall Law students will participate in a civil rights clerk-ship program throughout the South this summer. Sponsored by the Law Students Civil Rights Research Council, they will be working as part of a team of 120 students from leading law schools in the nation." Inevitably such students will modify the ethos of the legal profession.

Likewise, doctors have not been noted for a disposition to contravene the status quo in American society. The general stodginess and the lack of intellectual vivacity in this profession are among the reasons why many of the more intelligent and discerning undergraduates in recent years have chosen academic or research careers in various biological sciences in preference to attending medical school. Countervailing tendencies may be found—Dr. Benjamin Spock's public pronouncements on foreign policy, for example, or doctors' picketing the International Automobile Show in New York on behalf of greater automobile safety.[9] But medical schools will recapture their share of the best undergraduate students only to the extent that they can appeal to their humanitarian instincts and emphasize the need for their social contributions.

One has but to skim the marriage columns in *The New York Times* to see that a very high proportion of the well-educated sons and daughters of businessmen and industrialists do not enter business and industry. A surprising number are pursuing academic careers or are preparing for such. On the other hand, few sons and

[9] Physicians as Activists. *The Nation,* May 3, 1965, **200,** 463.

daughters of professional men and of those in academic pursuits seem disposed to enter business and industry. Research carried out by David Beardslee and Donald O'Dowd[10] indicates that liberal arts college students think businessmen less intelligent and more selfish than professional men. They also see them as less emotionally stable. Does this mean that control of business and industry will pass gradually to more narrowly educated and less sophisticated individuals?

The education of women may recapture the innovative spirit it formerly possessed.[11] At the very time that automation, cybernation, and attendant economic and social changes are likely to produce widespread unemployment, increased leisure time, and redefinition of work versus leisure, college women and alumnae are encouraged by educators to realize themselves in the world of work after the manner of men. The situation is similar to that of the Negro in the United States. Now that there is little place for youth in the work force, Negro high school students are urged to take advantage of educational opportunities and thereby qualify for good jobs after graduation. Thus far, educated women have had the good sense not to enter male professions and occupations en masse. They seem to recognize instinctively that there are more rewarding activities than the weary and uninteresting rounds that men have been pursuing for generations. New ways of living and of working are now needed, and educated women, free as they are from some of the traditional commitments of men, are in a unique position to provide them.

A discipline and a profession of college teacher or educator will emerge. It is ridiculous to suppose that a graduate degree in one field of study or another is sufficient qualification for educating college students. A teacher should also know something about college students, how and what they learn, how they are changed by educational experiences, and the like.

Many research workers in the social sciences have not been interested in the study of whole human beings in real-life situations,

[10] Beardslee, David, and O'Dowd, Donald. Students and the Occupational World. In Sanford (Ed.). *The American College.*

[11] See Chapter 11.

but the need to understand college students may change this attitude. A classic example is the situation at the University of California. Although thousands upon thousands of students have served as research subjects for studies and experiments in the School of Education and in the Departments of Sociology and Psychology, research workers were generally not concerned with students as students or as complex human beings. Students were simply eyes for perception experiments, ears for auditory experiments, or representatives of this or that reference group. The turmoil at Berkeley suddenly galvanized a number of research workers into looking at their student colleagues as whole people.

Will educators be interested in accurate and useful information about students and college experience as it becomes available? A year ago I would not have thought so. The attitude of most administrators and faculty members toward educational research was negative. They were disposed to dismiss such research as the product of second-rate thinking that leads to emphasis on life adjustment or driver education at the expense of "real" education. But current student unrest may well change these views and impress upon educators the necessity for systematic observation and empirical study. Rhetoric about the glories and wonders of college education will no longer suffice. There will be much more interest in what actually goes on.

I do not suggest that my description of students is appropriate to the majority of American undergraduates. Most of them are conventional, bound by the traditional demands of American society and culture, dutiful, and complaisant. The students I have described represent an avant-garde at the more prestigious colleges; but what is a ripple today may well be a wave tomorrow. Man and his society are complex, and I hardly believe that human progress is inevitable. I am convinced, nevertheless, that if we can refrain from blowing ourselves up in the next decade or so, many of the educational and social changes that I have described will come to pass.

14

New Alignments of Power and Authority

In the modern world, social changes that evolved slowly over long periods of time in former eras now take place in generations, decades, or even years. American higher education offers an excellent illustration. Events of the last few years have rendered invalid or at least questionable beliefs that five or ten years ago seemed to be unassailable truths.

Until very recently, no description of a college or university campus by an educator or social scientist was complete without some reference to the two cultures, faculty culture and student culture. Faculty culture represented the values of liberal education—regard for the life of the mind, independence of judgment, intellectual curiosity, and the like. Student culture represented a compromise between the values of liberal education and those of the wider society. The passage of a student through college could be viewed as a process of partial socialization into the faculty culture. A freshman entered college imbued with the traditional or conventional values and ways of thought of the home and the home community. During the college years, he modified these values and ways of thought in the direction of faculty beliefs and outlook. This process was mediated for lower classmen by upper division students who served as models for the kinds of changes that were expected of them.

Student culture reconciled the values of the faculty and those of society at large, because too much change would be dysfunctional in the lives of most students. Students had to leave college and enter the world of business and the professions. They could not permit themselves to become so alienated from their parents' world that they could not return to it with some degree of equanimity. Student culture very neatly succeeded in socializing students well enough to meet faculty demands and yet not so well that their education rendered return to families and communities difficult or impossible. In this process, the faculty wielded the power; students were, in a sense, a subject people.[1] They preserved their integrity by giving in only to the extent that they had to. In subtle ways, student norms limited the control of the faculty. These norms dictated the amount of academic work to be done by students, the kinds of contacts students were to have with the faculty, and the like.[2] This is not to say, of course, that all students were controlled uniformly by a monolithic student culture. Exceptions and individual vagaries were numerous. But by and large, most students took guidance and direction from this student culture, which was designed to incorporate and at the same time to limit faculty influence.

Recent events are making this two-culture model obsolete. The image of the faculty's trying to stir up a complacent student body is hardly appropriate on many campuses. Further, likening students to a kind of subject people does not jibe with many recent developments. The clash of faculty and student cultures is a metaphor that has lost much of its relevance.

Coleridge's "willing suspension of disbelief" is surely required to appreciate what is taking place on many campuses today. At Berkeley, the Select Committee of the Academic Senate has been examining almost every aspect of the educational scene. The report

[1] See Bushnell, John H. Student Culture at Vassar. In Sanford (Ed.). *The American College.*

[2] Freedman. The Passage Through College; Becker *et al. Boys in White.*

of this committee has recently been published.[3] The faculty of Cornell has completed a series of reports concerned with various aspects of undergraduate education at that university. One of the many recommendations made by the Committee on the Quality of Undergraduate Instruction is ". . . that the university give Student Government financial and technical assistance in preparing and publishing competent and responsible campus-wide student evaluation of courses."[4] At the City College of New York, the administration is lending official support to a survey of student attitudes toward courses and instructors. President Brewster has proposed that procedures be instigated which will give students some influence over tenure decisions at Yale. As *The Harvard Crimson* commented on this recommendation, "The plan is a cautious one, but simply by recognizing that a problem exists, it is momentous."[5]

President Edward D. Eddy, Jr., of Chatham College has recommended a voice for students in establishing educational policy. "Every college and university committee," he said, "ought to include voting student members."[6] E. K. Fretwell, Jr., President of the Association for Higher Education of the National Education Association, has made similar statements.[7] The American Association of University Professors has published a document which has been described as a "bill of rights" for students.[8] At San Francisco State College, a sizable number of student-inspired courses have been added to the curriculum. These courses tend to be interdisciplinary in nature. They focus on such matters as community involvement, artistic and aesthetic experiences that are not available

[3] Academic Senate, University of California. *Education at Berkeley: Report of the Select Committee on Education.* Berkeley, Calif.: University of California, 1966.

[4] Report of the Faculty Committee on the Quality of Undergraduate Instruction. Ithaca, New York: 1965, p. 29 (Mimeographed).

[5] Fallout from Berkeley. *The Harvard Crimson,* October 26, 1965, p. 2.

[6] Eddy, Edward D., Jr. Quoted in Student Voice in College Policy Is Urged. *The Washington Post,* October 7, 1965, p. 7.

[7] Fretwell, E. K., Jr. Quoted in Educators Urged to Heed Students. *The New York Times,* June 29, 1965, p. 25.

[8] Committee S on Faculty Responsibility for the Academic Freedom of Students. Statement on the Academic Freedom of Students. *Bulletin of the American Association of University Professors,* Winter 1965, **51,** 447–449.

to students in other courses, political and philosophical concepts and their relationships to current events, and self-knowledge.

This is not to say that students have established dominion over college and university campuses. It has been the genius of the "Establishment" in the United States to yield somewhat in the face of strong pressure. A good way of limiting and hence coming to terms with a rebellious movement is to incorporate some of the principles or activities of the rebellion. Doubtless this is happening in the case of student protest and criticism. If students are brought into the Establishment, they are not likely to press their case so forcibly as when they were on the outside. It seems reasonable to conclude that to some extent the conciliatory attitude toward students that is so widespread on the national scene represents what the psychoanalysts call "defense by partial incorporation."

But surely this is not all that is involved. Fundamental shifts in allegiances and alignments and in channels and hierarchies of authority have occurred. The former divorce between faculty and students is now being transformed into a divorce between colleges and universities and the wider society. Consider the phenomenon of opposition to the American military involvement in Vietnam. This opposition is very much centered among intellectuals and academics. Students and faculty tend to be united in this struggle. They are allies, not antagonists. I do not wish to exaggerate the extent of opposition among students to the situation in Vietnam. Most students are not disposed to oppose official American policy. I am certain, however, that rebellious tendencies are on the increase. The unity of students and faculty members in opposition to various aspects of American life or public programs will grow. Among John Dewey's many criticisms of American education was the tendency of educational institutions to reflect the larger society rather than to put pressure on that society to change. At least as far as higher education is concerned, students and faculty are taking a leaf from Dewey's books.

A teach-in concerned with Vietnam, or a civil rights activity in which students and faculty work together on a more or less equal basis, is but one facet of the beginnings of drastic alteration in status and authority relationships in American colleges and universities. The presence of students at faculty meetings or on faculty committees is another example. The origination of ideas for courses among students is a third. A fourth is the growing movement to reduce the rigors and pressure of grades, as, for example, by the use of a pass-fail grading procedure outside the major field. These and similar developments indicate that relationships between faculty and students based on dominance and subordination are on the way out. Such relationships are moving steadily in the direction of equalitarianism and cooperative endeavor, in which status considerations are minimal. Students are still more disposed to emulate faculty rather than vice versa, but the tendency for faculty members to take their cue from students is increasing.

This shift toward equalitarian relationships between faculty and students is part of a much larger trend in western societies.[9] Subject nations—African states, for example—are attaining freedom. Subject groups, Negroes in particular, are beginning to receive full human rights. In poverty programs and neighborhood redevelopment programs, the advice and counsel of the people at whom the programs are directed are sought. Ex-convicts are being trained to serve as parole officers. Rehabilitated drug addicts are helping individuals who are addicted to "kick" the habit. One can only conclude that a profound change in relationships between leaders and followers, between experts and novices, between teachers and students is taking place.

Casting a jaundiced eye in the direction of authority is a widespread phenomenon during the college years in the United States. In former years, this "rebellious independence" led to a clash between the youth world and the adult world—separate student and faculty cultures, for example. Nowadays the disposition on the part of adults to meet youth halfway is growing, at least on college and university campuses. Certain great observers and critics of social movements in the western world—Alexis de Tocqueville, Sören Kierkegaard, and Sigmund Freud, for example—have ex-

[9] "The demand of youth for a share in the reform of the universities is part of a larger demand for the achievement of democratic rights and the reconstruction of society through education." Taylor, Harold. American Idealism. *Saturday Review,* June 26, 1965, 14–16.

pressed wariness of such trends toward reduction of the status and power of authority. They have feared that anarchy and the breakdown of the moral order would occur.

Time alone will tell what the rapprochement between faculty and students will bring. It may presage the birth of new ways of life and thought or, on the contrary, a decline in the western academic and intellectual tradition. I myself tend toward optimism on this score. For example, to my way of thinking, the growing equalitarianism on college and university campuses has considerable value in the development of new knowledge and new ways of looking at things. In this process, the role of the authority or the expert can be almost a handicap. The person who is committed to the mastery of one discipline or to certain approaches to learning or scholarship may find difficulty in looking at things in new ways. The flexibility of youth, the sensitivity of young people to new experience, may well serve as an antidote to the artificial fragmentation of knowledge. In this light, the disposition on the part of some faculty to include students as coadjutors in educational activities has much functional value. Young people who possess greater sensitivity to the needs of society and the kinds of changes that are occurring in society can furnish some of this new direction in higher education.

Many students and faculty members are now beginning to recognize the true barriers to change in colleges and universities—for example, graduate education as exemplified by the doctoral dissertation, and the "publish or perish" system of awarding tenure and promotions to faculty. For too long, college presidents and other administrators have been cast as the villains of the piece. At times, of course, they have indeed stood in the way of change; but all too often, they have simply been scapegoats. They have been the objects of criticism that would have been more appropriately directed elsewhere—that is, toward specialization of knowledge increasingly divorced from meaning and synthesis.

Nevitt Sanford has cast a penetrating eye on this phenomenon.

> The kind of specialization of which we have been speaking is embodied in its purest form in the research professor working on the frontiers of knowledge with advanced graduate students and

> postdoctoral scholars. He provides the ideal for the rest of the faculty who fight for conditions of appointment that will come as close to his as possible. The undergraduate is left out not only because the faculty's interest is elsewhere, but because the specializations of knowledge and the professional language require a long, often dull period of mastery before the student can share the professor's concerns. . . . Specialization has even deeper implications for the student; it tends toward the fragmentation of *him.* When everything in nature is conceived as being susceptible to abstraction from its context for purposes of intensive study the student himself does not escape; he too is conceived as an aggregate of part-processes. . . .[10]

As long as this specialized conception of graduate education dominates colleges and universities, such reforms as take place can be only palliative.

The role of graduate students in the evolutionary processes I have been describing will be important. Graduate students serve as a link between faculty and undergraduate students. In former times, graduate students were junior-grade faculty. They had been recruited into the ranks of adult professionals, and they identified with these adults and began to act like them in short order. The gulf between graduate and undergraduate students was wide. Things are different now. A striking feature of the difficulties at Berkeley in 1964 and in fall 1966 was the extent to which graduate and undergraduate students had a common cause. The graduate students, many of them teaching assistants, turned away from father, as it were, and aligned themselves with little brother.

Nowadays large proportions of undergraduate students go on to graduate school. On some of the more prestigious campuses, this figure exceeds 80 per cent. In this situation the undergraduate and graduate currents merge into a continuous stream. Likewise, when one considers the increasing numbers of graduate students who enter some variant of academic life, the channels between undergraduate and faculty life seem very continuous. The trend toward

[10] Sanford, Nevitt. The Human Problems Institute and General Education. In Creativity and Learning. *Daedalus,* Summer 1965, **94,** 11.

rapprochement between faculty and students may to a considerable extent be due to the large number of young faculty members who have flooded the campuses in the last few years. They are close to their graduate and undergraduate student origins, and they are close to their students. The clash of cultures that is now most evident on many campuses is that between older faculty, over forty-five or thereabouts, on the one hand, and younger faculty, graduate students, and undergraduate students, on the other. Exceptions are numerous, of course, but by and large the faculty who are involved in activities like teach-ins are rather young.

In the near future, I look for little strife over intracollege and university issues. Relationships between the college and the society at large will not be so smooth, however.[11] I foresee many conflicts —over Vietnam, the draft, civil rights, the use of drugs, and many other issues. Faculty members and students will have some allies in these conflicts—liberal politicians and clergymen, for example. But most of American society will be arrayed against them. This discord could become very intense. For example, should American involvement in Vietnam be intensified, the forces that would like to silence critics in colleges and universities will gather strength. I foresee considerable possibility of a return to the repressiveness of the McCarthy era, with this difference—that the colleges and universities will fight back, and will not roll over and play dead as most of them did during the Korean War. There may be some hard times ahead.

[11] Such controversy will be reflected within colleges and universities, of course—as, for example, in disputes between "liberal" or "radical" students versus those who are more kindly disposed to the status quo.

Acknowledgments

Some of the chapters in *The College Experience* are based on previously published research. Those articles have been revised, but the content has not been substantially changed. "Personality Development in the College Years" (originally entitled "Personality Growth in the College Years") is reprinted with permission from the Spring 1965 *College Board Review* published by the College Entrance Examination Board, New York. "The Problem of Identity" (originally entitled "Some Theoretical and Practical Implications of a Longitudinal Study of College Women") appeared in *Psychiatry,* 1963, *26,* 176–187. "The College and the Image of Man" (originally entitled "The Men's Colleges and the Image of Man") is reprinted with permission from the *AAUW Journal,* March 1964, 107–110; and "The Future of the Women's College" (originally entitled "On the Future of the Women's Colleges: A Man's View") is reprinted with permission from the *AAUW Journal,* March 1963, 109–111. For permission to use my copyrighted material I wish to thank the following organizations. The Merrill-Palmer Institute for "A Longitudinal Study of Personality Development in College Alumnae," *Merrill-Palmer Quarterly,* 1963, *9,* 295–302; and for "The Sexual Behavior of American College Women: An Empirical Study and an Historical Survey," *Merrill-Palmer Quarterly,* 1965, *11,* 33–48. The American College Personnel Association for "The Role of the

Educated Woman: An Empirical Study of the Attitudes of a Group of College Women," *Journal of College Student Personnel,* 1965, *6,* 145–155. The Nation Associates, Inc., for "Roots of Student Discontent," *The Nation,* July 14, 1965, *200,* 639–643; and for "Turned On and Tuned Out," *The Nation,* January 31, 1966, 125–127. The Association for Higher Education, National Education Association, for "New Alignments of Power and Authority in Colleges and Universities," *Current Issues in Higher Education,* 1966, 149–153. The Society for the Psychological Study of Social Issues for "Changes in Six Decades of Some Attitudes and Values Held by Educated Women." *Journal of Social Issues,* 1961, *17,* 19–28.

Index

Y